# Educationally Correct, Academically Sound

## Fueling School Programs And Student Achievement

Brenda Sanders

ROWMAN & LITTLEFIELD EDUCATION
A division of
ROWMAN & LITTLEFIELD PUBLISHERS, INC.
Lanham • New York • Toronto • Plymouth, UK

Published by Rowman & Littlefield Education
A division of Rowman & Littlefield Publishers, Inc.
A wholly owned subsidiary of The Rowman & Littlefield Publishing Group, Inc.
4501 Forbes Boulevard, Suite 200, Lanham, Maryland 20706
www.rowman.com

10 Thornbury Road, Plymouth PL6 7PP, United Kingdom

Copyright © 2012 by Brenda Sanders

*All rights reserved.* No part of this book may be reproduced in any form or by any electronic or mechanical means, including information storage and retrieval systems, without written permission from the publisher, except by a reviewer who may quote passages in a review.

British Library Cataloguing in Publication Information Available

**Library of Congress Cataloging-in-Publication Data**

Sanders, Brenda, 1964- author.
Educationally correct, academically sound : fueling school programs and student achievement / Brenda Sanders.
p. cm.
Includes bibliographical references and index.
ISBN 978-1-4758-0000-5 (cloth : alk. paper) -- ISBN 978-1-4758-0001-2 (pbk. : alk. paper) -- ISBN 978-1-4758-0002-9 (electronic) (print)
1. School improvement programs--United States. 2. Academic achievement--United States. 3. Educational leadership--United States. I. Title.
LB2822.82.S26 2012
371.2'07--dc23

2012014051

This book is dedicated to God, and the two Margarets in my life: My mother and my daughter. This book is also dedicated to my big sister, Judy, who I never stopped looking up to.

# Contents

| | |
|---|---|
| Acknowledgments | vii |
| 1  Introduction | 1 |
| **I: Cooperativeness—The C in CAB** | **7** |
| 2  School-wide Guiding Philosophy | 9 |
| 3  Collaborative Relationships | 29 |
| 4  Family/School/Community Connections | 39 |
| **II: Accountability—The A in the CAB Model** | **45** |
| 5  Staff Accountability | 47 |
| **III: Boundlessness—The B in the CAB Model** | **59** |
| 6  Data-driven School-wide Evaluation | 61 |
| **IV: The Inception of CAB** | **67** |
| 7  The History of CAB | 69 |
| References | 83 |
| Index | 87 |

# Acknowledgments

First of all, I would like to acknowledge and thank God for seeing me when no one else does. I thank God for His faithfulness and for giving me the ability to write this book.

I would like to thank the two Margarets in my life: My mother and my daughter. Thank you, Moma and Margie for your unfailing Faith in me. I would like to thank my big sister Judy for being my first hero.

Thank you to Jenny Wilkinson for always having an encouraging word. Thank you to all of the educators who were willing to read my drafts and give feedback. I especially thank Rhonda Turner for taking the time to help me edit this book.

Lastly, I would like to thank Tom Koerner, Ph.D., vice president and editorial director at Rowman & Littlefield, for being patient with me during my sister's illness and seeing the potential in my work during the development stage.

## Chapter One

# Introduction

Welcome to "Educationally Correct, Academically Sound." Join the author on a tour as educators take a glimpse at their schools through the eyes of what research says about high performing schools. As a revitalization tool for educators, this book takes leaders on a journey of renewal, recovery, or enhancement depending on the needs of the individual institution.

Take the voyage and see school programs, operations, and configurations in a new light. Readers embark upon an adventure that shows staff how to bring all the pieces of an institution together to achieve optimal performance. The voyage begins with a brief glance at the map of this exploration. Let's call this map, CAB. See table 1.1 at the end of this chapter for the research CAB was derived from.

Each of the letters on the map stands for a different concept or section that will be visited. Within each concept lie characteristics that can be explored. The *C*, for instance, stands for cooperativeness and consists of three chapters of exploration including school-wide guiding philosophy (chapter two), collaborative relationships (chapter three), and family/school/community connections (chapter four).

Often, there is a disconnect among vision and mission statements, school operations, afterschool programs and curriculum decisions made at education establishments. In order to move schools into the twenty-first century, Chapter two will show educators how to create useable vision and mission statements as well as mission objectives that will be used to direct the school's daily operations, programs, and curriculum decisions.

At the core of any school is the ability of all school participants to work together to realize student achievement. In chapter three, educators journey on a road that leads to building collaborations: student, volunteer, and staff. This chapter discusses how to assign well-defined roles to students, volunteers, and staff so everyone involved will know what is expected of them. Chapter three also illustrates how to set up protocols for decision making within collaborative efforts so the goals of collaborative efforts can be attained.

The importance of making families and the community an integral part of the school community can never be overstated. Chapter four gives strategies on how to connect to and recruit family and community members. This includes those who work during the day, those who do not, those who are literate and those who are educated.

Now, it is time to look at the *A* section of the map. The *A* section corresponds to accountability, which looks at leadership, staff and then student accountability. It consists of chapter five, which focuses on what leadership and teachers need to do in order to put a checks-and-balances system in place for students. Chapter five also concentrates on how to ensure that curriculum aligns with standards, as well as how to connect staff development to classroom learning.

Additionally, chapter five suggests the following ways that teachers can switch paradigms:

1. Take full responsibility for student learning.
2. Set high standards for students.
3. Provide a means to meet the standards by scaffolding students to high achievement.

Finally, it is time to visit the last section of the map, the *B* section. *B* targets *boundlessness*, data-driven evaluation. The details of boundlessness will be discussed in chapter six of the book.

In schools embracing boundlessness, everyone learns. In order to accomplish this task of continuous growth and learning, chapter six illustrates how to utilize data to inform student achievement and staff development. It discusses the importance of training staff in how to use data effectively.

The final chapter discusses the background of CAB. CAB was derived from a literature review as part of the author's doctoral dissertation. This chapter focuses on each of the letters in CAB individually. The meaning of each of the letters will be explored. Chapter seven gives a summary of the letters in the acronym as well as how CAB originated.

Chapter seven is the last chapter, as opposed to the first, because the point of the book is to illustrate how CAB can be utilized in a practical manner in educational institutions. The last chapter is simply for background purposes while table 1.1 offers the research base upon which CAB was originated.

Key points at the beginning of each chapter have been added to make it easy for the reader to search out specific information. The only exception is the last chapter. Additionally, chapter summaries at the end of each chapter will give a general idea about the details of the chapter.

Table 1.1 CAB Table

| *(CAB)* | *Cooperativeness* | *Accountability* | *Boundlessness* |
|---|---|---|---|
| *Sanders, 2010* | School-wide guiding philosophy, collaborative relationships, family/school/community connections | student staff | data-driven evaluation |
| *Reeves, 2000* | collaborative scoring of student work | clear curriculum choices, emphasis on nonfiction writing | focus on academic achievement, frequent assessment of student progress and multiple opportunities for improvement |
| *Marzano, 2003* | parent and community involvement | guaranteed and viable curriculum, safe and orderly environment, collegiality and professionalism, instructional strategies, classroom management, curriculum design, learned intelligence and background knowledge, student motivation | challenging goals and effective feedback |
| *Scheerens, & Bosker, 1997* | parental involvement, cooperative working environment | focus on achievement, creating a safe and orderly climate, focused curriculum, strong leadership, time on task | monitoring of student progress |
| *Daggett, 2005* | community involvement, home environment, | programs that stretch students well beyond the core academic skills measured by state and national tests | high academic performance in core areas as measured on state and national tests, social and personal development |

| | | | |
|---|---|---|---|
| *Lein, Johnson, & Ragland, 1997* | collaborative problem solving, sense of family, collaboration and trust | academic success for all students, no excuses | careful experimentation, passion for learning and growing |
| *Hair, Craft, & Allen, 2001* | instructional leadership and faculty collaboration | the principal and entire staff have a strong sense of efficacy, standards-based instruction was pervasive, all schools had excellent school-wide discipline, student learning was the school's greatest priority | a variety of approaches to professional learning are present, the schools spent a great deal of time and attention on data analysis, the entire faculty demonstrated great flexibility in trying different approaches to meet student needs |
| *US Department of Education (USDE), 1999* | collaboration on instructional time, partnership with parents | focus on servicing kids, accountability for students/teachers, instruction, standards, and assessments aligned, daily instructional time maximized | work on one goal at a time, keep going regardless of setbacks |
| *Picucc et al, 2002* | collaborative environments | high expectations for all schools, support students by any means necessary | data-driven improvement in teaching and learning |
| *Craig et al., 2005* | school/family connections, shared leadership, shared goals for learning | learning culture, effective teaching, aligned and balanced curriculum | purposeful student assessment |

| | | | |
|---|---|---|---|
| Ellis et al., 2004 | unified practice supported by targeted professional development | curriculum alignment with the MA frameworks, effective systems to support curriculum alignment, emphasis on inclusion and access to the curriculum, a well disciplined academic and social environment, access to resources to support key initiatives, effective staff recruitment, retention, and deployment, flexible leaders and staff, effective leadership | use of student assessment data to inform decision-making |
| Shields, et al., 1995 | collaborative culture | focus on learning | opportunities for capacity building |
| Joint Legislative Audit Review Commission (JLARC), 2004 | teamwork, collaboration, and vertical integration | strong, stable leadership; environment conducive to learning; effective teaching staff; curriculum alignment, pacing and resources; differentiation in teaching; academic remediation; structure, and intensity of school day | data-driven assessment of student weaknesses and teacher effectiveness |

# *I*

# Cooperativeness — The C in CAB

Cooperativeness exemplifies the school's intention to give everyone connected to the school an opportunity to participate in or contribute to some aspect of the institution in a meaningful way. It embodies administrators, staff, the community, parents, and students working together to achieve the ultimate goal of student achievement.

Specifically, cooperativeness incorporates the following three concepts: school-wide guiding philosophy (shared vision), collaborative relationships, and family/school/community connections. Section 1 highlights each of these concepts in individual chapters.

*Chapter Two*

# School-wide Guiding Philosophy

## KEY POINTS

School-wide guiding philosophy

- 3 essential purposes
    - Creates common purpose
    - Maintains focus
    - Creates a pattern of unity
- Aligns with school programs, curriculum, and operations
- Use vision and mission statements to create school-wide guiding philosophy
- The vision statement
    - Should be done cooperatively
    - Creates buy-in
    - Helps stakeholders understand school's daily mission
    - Questions to consider
    - Does it embody the school's vision of a perfect school?
    - Does the vision have a global or societal perspective?
    - Is it results oriented?
- The mission statement
    - Questions to consider
    - Does it embody what the school wants to accomplish daily?
    - Does it signify the goals of the vision statement?
    - Are the goals at an individual and/or building level?
    - Is it results oriented?
- Mission objectives
    - Directs the operations, programs, and curriculum decisions

o Questions to answer in each objective
-Who will be required to meet the objective?
-How many will be required meet the objective?
-What measure will be used to determine obtainment?
-What is the criterion for passing?
-What is the cut-off date for obtainment?
-Who will administer the measure?
-In what setting will the measure be administered?

Building cooperativeness within a school building begins with a strong foundation. Having a solid foundation, such as a well-crafted school-wide guiding philosophy gives any educational institution something concrete to build upon and operate in. Most schools already have a vision and/or mission statement. Unfortunately, many of these declarations go unused. As such, vision and mission statements remain disconnected from the school's daily operations defeating the purpose of the statements.

According to research, a school-wide guiding philosophy serves three purposes. First, the statement solidifies a common purpose, which means everyone in the building is working toward the same end. Secondly, having such a statement helps staff and leadership maintain focus during the institution's daily operations. Third, a school-wide guiding philosophy creates a pattern of unity.

School-wide guiding philosophies come in diverse forms. A social cause, for instance, can be used as a school's philosophy. A bill of rights or a school constitution can also be utilized as an institution's collective statement. Basically, any shared destination can be used as a mutual philosophy. However, it is important to note that using a uniform declaration does not replace the vision and mission statements. Rather, the organization's philosophy statement should stem from the vision and mission affirmations.

Vision and mission statements fail to meet their vital purpose in a school when the assertions do not direct the daily operations of the school. No mission or vision declaration should be done in isolation of the school's programs, operations, and goals. For this reason, vision and mission affirmations should be crafted or re-crafted in a way that declares the school's daily mission. Properly crafted vision and mission statements drive every decision that is made at the building level from staff development to discipline.

If a school's ultimate mission, for instance, is to create an environment of cooperativeness on every level, then it would follow that the school's discipline model might consist of class meetings where discipline issues were defined, consequences were set, multi-faceted discussions were encouraged, and resolutions were cooperatively determined.

# CRAFTING A VISION STATEMENT

A school-wide guiding philosophy starts with a vision statement. From the vision statement, the mission statement along with mission objectives should be crafted. Connecting the vision statement, mission statement and mission objectives to the school-wide guiding philosophy creates a single road map that all the entities in a school building follow. At the very least, teachers and administrators should collaborate on producing vision and mission statements.

Students, parents, and other stakeholders may also collaborate with staff to create these statements. Inviting all stakeholders to help develop vision and mission declarations along with the objectives can be rewarding, but very time-consuming. This level of participation can give parents and other stakeholders a sense of belonging to the school and a greater buy-in to the daily mission of the school.

Furthermore, stakeholders will understand what the school hopes to accomplish and be more willing to engage in the process of schooling alongside school staff. Allowing this level of cooperativeness will prove to be well worth it.

Utilize the following three steps as a guide to developing a vision statement. Remember that a vision statement signifies a general intention. Vision statements are not meant to be specific.

## Step One: Dream

A very close friend once told me that it doesn't take any more to dream a big dream than it does a small one. So, don't just dream. Dream big! In other words, think about how the school would operate if money or resources were not an issue. What would the perfect school look like or produce? Remember, there are no limitations other than those that are self-imposed. Take the time to write down the dreams that come out of this exercise.

Preferably, this is done as a cooperative effort. Write the dreams on a dry erase board or a flip chart, and categorize them into dominant themes. There will be many similarities. Consider the list of examples when one school leader first began thinking about that dream school and what it should represent:

1. The Academy is an enrichment opportunity equipping students with the tools to learn, while empowering learners with the knowledge to use the tools.
2. The Academy's students will be able to compete competently with students of the same age throughout the world in every academic area.

3. The Academy will mold students into independent learners who perform at grade level in all subjects, achieve passing scores on all standardized tests and believe that they can achieve their dreams.
4. The Academy will ensure student success in the twenty-first century through the issuance of laptops for every student.
5. The Academy will empower students to be successful through a mastery-based, individualized, authentic experience.
6. The Academy will foster a mindset in children to build a safe, morally responsible and respectful society.

## Step Two: Incorporate Results Only

It is normal to think in terms of how to get results, but for this exercise, let's focus on results only. The most common mistake in drafting these statements is failing to articulate what the end result looks like. Look at the list of dreams of the ideal school from step one. Change every dream into a result.

For right now, forget about how the dream will be accomplished, just concentrate on the results of the dreams. What is the end result for each dream? What will happen as a result of the dream? What is the point of the dream? This is how the school leader changed the dreams in step one into results-oriented goals:

1. The Academy is an enrichment opportunity equipping students with the tools to learn, while empowering learners with the knowledge to use the tools = literate, knowledgeable graduates.
2. The Academy students will be able to compete competently with students of the same age throughout the world in every academic area = students getting dream jobs.
3. The Academy will mold students into independent learners who perform at grade level in all subjects, achieve passing scores on all standardized tests and believe that they can achieve their dreams = no academic obstacles to success.
4. The Academy will ensure student success through the issuance of laptops for every student = students being computer fluent.
5. The Academy will empower students to be successful through a mastery-based individualized authentic experience = students have the ability to learn in any environment.
6. The Academy will foster a mindset in children to build a safe, morally responsible and respectful society = students who become respectful, morally responsible members of society.

## Step Three: Make Results Global

Because schools compete in a global arena, it is important for schools to start from the highest, which is the global or societal, perspective. What does the school want to accomplish in terms of preparing students for society or global competition? Or, what effect will the school or students have on society, or the world? Think global. Are all the dreams global? If not, change each dream to a global perspective.

Nothing is written in stone. Feel free to add to or change dreams at any time. This is also where the vision statement will be changed to include its final language. Be creative. Don't hold back. Consider how the school leader put all the result-oriented ideals together from step two to form a global/societal perspective. Then, look at how the final vision statement using global results was constructed.

1. literate, knowledgeable graduates = know what peers around the world know
2. students getting dream jobs = ability to compete in a global marketplace
3. no academic obstacles to success = capable of getting an Ivy League education
4. students being computer fluent = students have total World Wide Web capabilities
5. students have the ability to learn in any environment = ability to succeed at online learning, computer-based learning, service learning, face-to-face learning, and self-help learning
6. students become respectful, morally responsible members of society and work toward society being a respectful, morally responsible place to live = students become respectful morally responsible members of society and work toward helping the world to embrace these principles.

## Final Vision Statement

*The Academy has a vision that its students will leave the institution on a comparable academic level to peers around the globe, enabling students to compete in a global marketplace where graduates can realize their individual dreams. The Academy has a dream that its school will produce high school graduates capable of gaining an Ivy League education, possess overall capabilities in the utilization of the World Wide Web and have the skills to thrive in any learning environment. The Academy dreams that its students will help build a safe, morally responsible, respectful society in which every person is treated like a king or a queen.*

Now, consider how the vision statement was used to create a bill of rights for students which can be utilized as a school-wide guiding philosophy. See table 2.1. Notice how easy it is to create a school-wide guiding philosophy once the vision statement has been created. It is a natural progression.

## MISSION STATEMENT

With a vision statement in hand, the school's mission flows naturally from the vision. While the vision statement signifies a general global look at the ideal school, the mission statement consists of a more specific glance at the results educators want to see at the building and/or individual level.

Note that the individual can represent administrators, teachers, or students. What would it take at the building and/or individual level for the ideal vision to happen? Answer this question in terms of results at the building and/or individual level.

Table 2.1
Example of school-wide guiding philosophy stemming from vision statement

*Bill of Rights for Students*

- *WE, the students of The Academy,* have a right to acquire the knowledge, skills and competence we need to reach our dreams.
- *WE, the students of The Academy,* have a right to be treated with dignity and respect.
- *WE, the students of The Academy,* have a right to be in a classroom environment in which we can construct our own learning at our own pace.
- *WE, the students of The Academy,* have a right to be safe and secure.
- *WE, the students of The Academy,* have a right to hold an unpopular opinion.
- *We, the students of The Academy,* have a responsibility to behave in a morally responsible manner.
- *WE, the students of The Academy,* have a right to be excited about our Academy experience.
- *WE, the students of The Academy,* have a right to explore different learning environments.
- *WE, the students of The Academy,* have a right to be technologically advanced.
- *WE, the students of The Academy,* have a right to have the skills to compete with our peers around the world.

## Step One: Get Back in the Dream Mode

Yes, it is just as important to start drafting the mission statement in the dream mode as it was in creating the vision statement. Put limited thinking on the backburner so the ideal school can take root. If educators shift into reality mode, creative ideas will inherently be lost. Reality mode only allows the listing of things that the school has the money or resources to do. Dream mode encourages leaders to do what is needed to achieve success.

Whether resources are available or not, commit to doing what is necessary to succeed. Children in every school deserve at least that much. This may mean reallocating resources and money, but it also means finding new, more creative ways to solve old problems. Begin by separating the sentences in the vision statement the way this school leader did.

1. The Academy has a vision that its students will leave the institution on a comparable academic level to peers around the globe enabling students to compete in a global marketplace where graduates can realize their individual dreams.
2. The Academy has a dream that its school will produce high school graduates capable of gaining an Ivy League education, possess overall capabilities in the utilization of the World Wide Web and have the skills to thrive in any learning environment.
3. The Academy dreams that its students will help build a safe, morally responsible, respectful society in which every person is treated like a king or a queen.

## Step Two: Make Building and/or Individual Level List

Ask the following question: What will it take at the building and/or individual level to accomplish the tasks from the vision statement? Make a list of the answers for each sentence in the prior step. Consider the answers the school leader came up with when answering this question using the sentences from the vision statement in the prior step.

1. The Academy has a vision that its students will leave the institution on a comparable academic level to peers around the globe enabling students to compete in a global marketplace where graduates can realize their individual dreams = students must be independent learners, self-motivated, able to perform at grade level in all subjects as compared to peers around the globe, get comparable scores on the same standardized tests as peers around the globe, and extensively explore careers.
2. The Academy has a dream that its school will produce high school graduates with the capability of gaining an Ivy League education, possess overall capabilities in the utilization of the World Wide Web

and have the skills to thrive in any learning environment = students must engage in worldwide competitions with peers, produce research-based projects, learn computers/Internet, and master different learning environments.
3. The Academy has a dream that its students will help build a safe, morally responsible, respectful society in which every person is treated like a king or a queen = character education, community service, service learning projects, democracy modeled at institution.

## Step Three: Incorporate Results Only

Why would an organization need to know its destination prior to getting directions? Perhaps it is because the institution must know where it is going before a road map can be created to get there. Likewise, the mission statement generates a destination. As with the vision statement, the mission statement includes results only.

Mission statements basically declare the results educators want to see on a daily basis within their specific school building. The mission statement reminds administrators, staff and students of the shared goal the school endeavors to achieve. Look at the list derived from the prior step. Change each item on the list to a result. Some items may generate the same result. What will the end result look like at the building and/or individual level? Be specific. Consider how the school leader made the list results-oriented. Then look at how the final mission statement utilizing building/individual level results were constructed.

1. students must be independent learners, self-motivated, able to perform at grade level in all subjects as compared to peers around the globe, get comparable scores on the same standardized tests as peers around the globe, and extensively explore careers = independent learners who are able to perform at grade level in all subjects as compared to peers around the globe, get comparable scores on the same standardized tests as peers around the globe, and explore different careers
2. students must engage in worldwide competitions with peers, produce research-based projects, be technologically savvy, and master different learning environments = common software fluency, basic hardware fluency, competent researchers, World Wide Web mastery, and diverse learning environments mastery
3. character education, community service, service learning projects, democracy modeled at institution = community service requirement, school culture of character development, democracy modeled at school

## Final Mission Statement

*In a school culture of character development and democracy, The Academy is on a mission to mold students into being World Wide Web capable, software fluent, hardware proficient, research competent learners who perform at grade level in all subjects comparable to peers throughout the world. Students at the Academy will achieve scores comparable to peers around the globe on standardized tests, participate in community service, explore careers, and take part in "Fridays in Session," a shadow of democracy in society.*

A finely crafted mission statement can also be utilized as the school-wide guiding philosophy. However, for example purposes, the school-wide guiding philosophy will be a separate document. Because the school-wide guiding philosophy stems from the vision and mission statements, the document has been created along with these statements.

Notice that the school leader began crafting a student bill of rights (to be used as a school-wide guiding philosophy) from the vision statement. See table 2.1. Now, more will be added to the school-wide guiding philosophy to finalize the bill of rights since the mission statement has been completed. Let's revisit the bill of rights the school leader began upon the completion of the vision statement in table 2.1.

Try to keep the school-wide guiding philosophy document on one page. Manipulate the margin or change the font size to reduce it to one page if needed. Notice the few rights added from the mission statement. Please see table 2.2. Again, notice how easily the last three items stream from the mission statement.

Table 2.2
Example of final school-wide guiding philosophy

*Bill of Rights for Students*

- *WE, the students of The Academy,* have a right to acquire the knowledge, skills and competence we need to reach our dreams.
- *WE, the students of The Academy,* have a right to be treated with dignity and respect.
- *WE, the students of The Academy,* have a right to be in a classroom environment in which we can construct our own learning at our own pace.
- *WE, the students of The Academy,* have a right to be safe and secure.
- *WE, the students of The Academy,* have a right to hold an unpopular opinion.
- *WE, the students of The Academy,* have a responsibility to behave in a morally, responsible manner.

- *WE, the students of The Academy,* have a right to be excited about our Academy experience.
- *WE, the students of The Academy,* have a right to explore different learning environments.
- *WE, the students of The Academy,* have a right to be software fluent, hardware proficient, World Wide Web capable, and research competent.
- *WE, the students of The Academy,* have a right to be able to compete with our peers around the world.
- *WE, the students of The Academy,* have a right to opportunities that allow us to build our character as an individual.
- *WE, the students of The Academy,* have a right to explore different careers.
- *WE, the students of The Academy,* have a right to be in a learning environment that provides opportunity for students to shadow democracy in society.

## MISSION OBJECTIVES

Now that the vision and mission statements have been constructed, the mission objectives will flow naturally. Utilize the mission statement to form the mission objectives. Begin by dividing the mission statement into objectives. Consider the following list of objectives derived from the mission statement. Notice that the objectives resemble the final goals of the mission statement. Do not hesitate to add or eliminate results at any time during the process.

### Step One: List Mission Objectives

1. common software fluency, hardware proficiency, World Wide Web capable, competent researchers, perform at grade level in all subjects comparable to peers throughout the world, achieve scores comparable to peers around the globe on standardized tests, explore careers
2. community service requirement, school culture of character development, democracy modeled at school

### Step Two: Articulate Who Is Expected to Meet Objectives

Who will be expected to achieve the mission objectives? It is essential to specify who is expected to meet the standards as well as how many or what percentage of the population is expected to achieve this objective. By when will this objective be completed? Determine a cut-off date for obtainment of each objective. Add the "who will do what by when" to each objective on the list in the above step. Look at how the school leader added this information to the mission objectives:

1. One hundred percent of students attending The Academy will perform at grade level in all subjects comparable to peers throughout the world within three years of attending The Academy.
2. One hundred percent of students attending The Academy will achieve scores comparable to peers throughout the world within at least the average range for their age/grade level on standardized tests within the second year of attendance reaching the eightieth percentile within five years of attending The Academy.
3. One hundred percent of students attending The Academy will complete a yearly career exploration program which includes at least two hours a week in a career related internship.
4. One hundred percent of students attending The Academy will complete at least two hours a week of community service related to a theme consistent with the semester character building theme.
5. One hundred percent of students attending The Academy will experience ongoing character building.
6. One hundred percent of students attending The Academy will serve in different capacities on an ongoing basis as part of our school community's democratic society.
7. One hundred percent of students attending The Academy will be required to engage in an assignment once a week that entails skillfully surfing the Internet to complete the assignment.
8. One hundred percent of students attending The Academy will become common-software fluent within two years of attending The Academy.
9. One hundred percent of students attending The Academy will become basic-hardware fluent within one year of attending The Academy.
10. One hundred percent of students attending The Academy will become competent researchers within two years of attending The Academy.
11. One hundred percent of students attending The Academy will be required to engage in a computer-based learning environment to learn a skill or do an assignment (online learning, CD learning, interactive computer games, tutorials) at least once a week.

## Step Three: Determine How Objectives Will Be Measured

Since the standard for achievement has been set, there is but one question: How will administrators, staff, and/or students know when a specific standard has been met? Choose a measurement that will show to what extent the objective has been met. It makes no sense to go through the process of writing up mission objectives if the success or failure of the objective cannot be measured.

In writing mission objectives, commit to working toward the standards already set. Knowing how it will look upon achievement of a goal is just as important as having a plan to get there. Do not just include the measurement. Include the criteria for passing.

Also, settle on who will assess achievement and in what setting will assessment take place. Will the teacher be the evaluator? Or, will there be an outside source that evaluates whether mission objectives have been obtained. Where will the evaluation take place? Be sure to answer all of these questions within the mission objectives. Consider the following examples of mission objectives and how the objectives will be measured using the objectives in the above step.

**Final Mission Objectives**

1. One hundred percent of students attending The Academy will perform at grade level in all subjects comparable to peers throughout the world within three years of attending The Academy as indicated by teachers surveying student portfolio records at the end of each semester and comparing to peer groups.
2. One hundred percent of students attending The Academy will achieve scores comparable to peers throughout the world within at least the average range for their age/grade level on standardized tests within the second year of attendance reaching the eightieth percentile within five years of attending The Academy as reported to the institution by an educational testing service.
3. One hundred percent of students attending The Academy will complete a yearly career exploration program which includes at least two hours a week in a career related internship as indicated by internship sign-in sheets from employers and a yearly career project as indicated by an annual exploration fair hosted by a school planning or parent group.
4. One hundred percent of students attending The Academy will complete at least two hours a week of community service related to a theme consistent with the semester character building theme as indicated by community service records, accomplishments, and reflections. Community service providers will monitor and turn in community service records noting accomplishments. Teachers will collect community service reflections.
5. One hundred percent of students attending The Academy will experience ongoing character building and score in at least the eightieth percentile on the assessment as indicated by end of semester character building assessments, reflections about classroom lessons learned, and

community service reflections. Teachers will give end of semester character building assessments, and collect reflections about classroom lessons learned.
6. One hundred percent of students attending The Academy will serve in different designated capacities on an ongoing basis as part of our school community's democratic society as evidenced by the school's "Fridays in Session."
7. One hundred percent of students attending The Academy will be required to engage in an assignment once a week that entails skillfully surfing the Internet to complete the assignment as indicated by scores on assignments turned in to teachers.
8. One hundred percent of students attending The Academy will become common software fluent scoring 80 percent within two years of attending The Academy as indicated by yearly computer-based, common-software fluency assessments. Students will take the tests on the computer when they feel they are ready. Scores that the students do not cancel will be retrieved by the teacher.
9. One hundred percent of students attending The Academy will become basic-hardware fluent scoring 80 percent within one year of attending The Academy as indicated by yearly computer-based basic hardware fluency assessment. Students will take the tests on the computer when they feel they are ready. Scores that the students do not cancel will be retrieved by the teacher.
10. One hundred percent of students attending The Academy will become competent researchers scoring 80 percent within two years of attending The Academy as indicated by yearly computer-based research competency assessment. Students will take the tests on the computer when they feel they are ready. Scores that the students do not cancel will be retrieved by the teacher.
11. One hundred percent of students attending The Academy will be required to engage in a computer-based learning environment to learn a skill or do an assignment (online learning, CD learning, interactive computer games, tutorials) at least once a week as indicated by scores turned in to teachers. Teachers will check mid-week to make sure students have planned learning a skill or doing an assignment through computer-based learning and turned in their scores.

Congratulations! The building blocks are in their respective places to secure a solid foundation. Everything in the organization should revolve around the school-wide guiding philosophy and mission objectives.

In other words, the school's professional learning communities (PLCs) should operate with the school-wide guiding philosophy and mission objectives as compasses to keep administrators and staff from getting off course or veering in the wrong direction. All of the school's operations, programs, decisions, and collaborations should be in line with the school-wide guiding philosophy and mission objectives since these documents represent the bottom line of the individual school.

Read the following interview excerpt of how a school leader used the school's mission objectives as their school-wide guiding philosophy. During the interview, the director addressed their mission statement and the six core objectives which serve as their school-wide guiding philosophy.

## EXCERPT FROM AN INTERVIEW WITH A SCHOOL ADMINISTRATOR

*Mission Statement*: To provide an educational setting tailored to the special needs of students who struggle to fulfill their potential in the traditional school environment. Through a nurturing and engaging educational community, students will gain knowledge, apply skills and become positive, knowledgeable and productive members of their local and global communities.

*Like all mission statements, it seems to be far-reaching, but that mission statement is a result of an effort by or input from students, staff, parents, and community members to simply put together what our mission is, what our objectives are. That mission that I stated earlier and those, kind of, core objectives are for the most part what drive what we do.*

*We as a team try to review that mission and those objectives annually, at the end of the year, both in retreat format or individual staff meetings to kind of gauge is that still our focus, is that what we are successful at or has our population changed or the demands changed that may require a change in our objectives or focus. So, that is kind of where we are at right now. It's a mission and objectives that we are definitely reviewing on a continual basis.*

*Core Objective 1*: Provide a safe, welcoming environment where individual, cultural and academic diversity is respected.

*We realize that our population is such that many of these kids will come from a variety of backgrounds. Particularly, the majority are low-income. While the cultural diversity may not be as broad as some of the other Portland schools, we have kids that are dealing with a number of family issues.*

*Also, some that have learning disabilities, social anxieties, educational disabilities, not severe, but enough that they were not successful in other environments. So, it's very important that we present an environment that is welcoming, and I think where you see that is in our staff and how they really provide respect and offer respect to all our kids.*

*None of our kids are judged on their past educational history, their family history, their economical level. We really do our best to make sure that not only in the atmosphere of the school, but also in the curriculum in the way that instruction is provided to kids, that it is welcoming, that kids feel safe, and that kids really feel that their particular situation, that they are valued and that the staff here is willing to go the extra mile to help them succeed.*

*I don't want to over-talk about the staff here, but I think if you were to spend, I say here, we're at the high school right now, but if you were to go to the middle school too, the staff, they are what make this program successful. I think you have to be a special kind of educator to really continue to do this and work with a real challenging population and to really draw the talents and the energy out of these kids when that has been limited in the past.*

Core Objective 2: Provide an inclusive school atmosphere that addresses various learning styles.

*It is important for us not to make it look like one group is different than the other. A good example of that is how we handle kids that are classified as special education or those who are on individual education plans. While we do have a special education teacher that is provided through the school district that works with these kids on modification, severe education plan, which is essentially some individual instruction. For the most part, we are inclusive. Our special education format is inclusive.*

*In other words, if you were to go into a classroom, you would not know who the special education students are because we work through the curriculum, through the design to make it fairly inclusive so those kids (do not feel) like they are separate in any way, that they're different, that they're less than successful or whatever. And it is very important to this population.*

*Again, because typically the history of non-success that those students have had in their traditional environment, whether it be for a learning disability, whether it be a social anxiety or a disability such as autism or attention deficit disorder, whatever it may be. If you were to go into one of our classrooms, you couldn't just easily pinpoint a kid that may be different or have a special program or be a part of special education. That's an example of how we treat our special education.*

Core Objective 3: Create a community of students and staff where education and individuals are important and valued.

*That's very important: how our staff addresses students. Part of, a big reason, why we are successful at what we do is that kids don't fall through the cracks here. They don't disappear like so many of the kids at the larger schools, whether it is a school of 2000 or classrooms of forty students. Students really can't be on their own here or fall through the cracks.*

*All of us teachers know kids by name, intimately. There is an advisory system that we have set up here where each teacher has a group of roughly fifteen kids that they are responsible for in monitoring their academic progress and, very importantly, staying in contact with the parent or guardian on a regular basis to make those parents aware of how their kids are doing both good and not so good.*

*And, we find that many of the parents for the first time, particularly at the high school level, are getting regular communication from their teacher or their student's teacher advisor on how their kid is doing, and it's really a relationship or a process where if you were to survey our parents, in which we did, we do annually, one of the biggest benefit they see to our program is the connections the students have made with their teachers and the parents have made with the teachers. Making those kids and parents feel valued and not just a school where their kids go.*

*Core Objective 4:* **Provide multiple opportunities to achieve high standards that ensure continuous improvement.**

*We feel that possibly unlike some of the traditional programs or larger programs, we recognize that we're going to get kids here at various times of their educational life. While there is a very high retention rate here, we do get kids sometimes that will come in mid-year, have left another school and have not been in school for a year.*

*It's important for us to really welcome them where they're at and not to say you, we are going to label you here because this is how you came in, but to really welcome them where they're at and do whatever we can to provide the opportunities for them to succeed and to graduate and to move onto a post-secondary education option or to prepare for the workforce right away.*

*That could mean that a student will oftentimes, sometimes, be here beyond the traditional four years because we can't control where the kids are at before they come to us. So, we will often get kids and we are somewhat selective, but we will get kids that may be a senior on paper or a junior on paper, but will need additional time and opportunities to get their diploma and be in a position to succeed beyond School X. We also, as the objective says, provide multiple opportunities.*

*There's always a continual learning process that goes on, and that kids, if something, a "standard," is not met in an expected time in a traditional environment, we will provide local opportunities to achieve that standard. I should say we're not going to keep someone here for seven years in a high school program before they leave, but our goal is to, again, accept those kids where they're at and, with the resources we have, provide as much opportunities for them to succeed.*

*Core Objective 5:* Address students' emotional needs that may be preventing academic success.

*We understand and recognize that our population inherently brings a variety of challenges that can be preventing their academic success. We have a large percentage of kids that come from single-parent households. The majority our kids are low income. Some are dealing with economic problems, family problems, drugs and alcohol problems. Some are dealing with death. We were surprised last year that at our high school, I don't know the exact percentages, but I think at one point, 20 percent of our population was dealing with either death of a parent or the impending death of a parent or close sibling.*

*We recognize that there are a lot of issues that affect the preparedness of our kids to be successful in school. Not only do all of our teachers serve as real good student advocates, but we have a licensed clinical social worker/ counselor at each location that works extensively with the students and families to address these issues that do prevent or stand in the way of academic success. If our personnel resources here cannot assist in that, then we are working very hard to link them up with support services in the community to assist in that effort.*

*Core Objective 6:* Build strong working relationships between parents, students, and educators.

*You heard about the three new R's in education: rigor, relevance, and*

*relationships. We can't get to the rigor with the relevance until strong relationships are built with our core populations which are the students and the parents. We just can't have that engagement, that success, until our staff has built strong relationships with our population. We work very hard at doing that.*

*Again, you will hear that from parents and students: what do you like most about (school x)? (They say) the staff, the teachers. Because when both the students and the parents have made that connection with our staff and that respect and that trust is there, the opportunity to succeed in the classroom is so much stronger than when you don't have that* (Sanders, 2009).

## CHAPTER SUMMARY

Chapter two expounds on the first concept found in cooperativeness: School-wide guiding philosophy. Its name encapsulates the meaning of the term perfectly. Administration, school staff, and students establish this philosophy to guide the daily operations of the institution. The school-wide guiding philosophy gives an educational institution a parameter to operate within. School decisions about curriculum, programs, or operations should always support the school-wide guiding philosophy.

The philosophy has three essential purposes within a school building: creates common purpose, maintains focus, and creates a pattern of unity. The document is created directly from the vision and mission statements.

Creating the vision statement is the first step in the process of setting up a school-wide guiding philosophy. The vision statement should be crafted cooperatively. Allowing all parties to participate has two important effects: It helps to create buy-in and helps stakeholders understand firsthand what the school hopes to accomplish.

There are three essential steps in crafting a vision statement. The school must first allow itself to think in terms of possibilities instead of realities. This means concentrating on what a school wants to do as opposed to what a school has the resources to do. This first step is crucial to being able to move past the status quo at any school to progress. Make a list of what the perfect school looks like or wants to produce.

The second step involves making the dream statements in step one results oriented. List the end result of each dream in step one. Stay in dream mode. Don't think about how it will happen right now. The last step in crafting a vision concentrates on making the list in step two global. What does the school want to accomplish in terms of preparing students for society or global competition? Change the dreams in step two to a global or societal perspective. Use the statements in step three to create the vision statement. Nothing is written in stone. Go back and change dreams at any time. Allow your creative juices to flow.

Utilize the vision statement to create the mission statement. It is important to do this so all aspects of schooling will be uniform. The mission statement needs to be specific. This statement sums up what educators want to achieve on a daily basis in a school building.

Follow three steps in generating a mission statement. Get back in dream mode, and commit to doing what it takes to achieve the ideal school. Don't worry about money at this time. The school can utilize new creative ways to solve old problems when the time comes. Start by numbering the sentences in the vision statement.

Step two focuses on listing the answers to the following question for each sentence in the vision statement: What will it take at the building and/or individual level to institute the goals of the vision statement? Step three concentrates on making the list in step two results oriented. Use the list in step three to produce the mission statement. Finalize the school-wide guiding philosophy once the mission statement is completed.

Ultimately, mission objectives must be generated from the mission statement. These mission objectives are as crucial to a school building as the school-wide guiding philosophy. School programs, curriculum, and operations should also align with mission objectives. Mission objectives are basically the goals of the mission statement. List the goals as a first step in creating the final objectives. Next, state what percentage of which population will be required to meet each objective (80 percent of students).

Specify when each objective has to be obtained by (the student's third semester). Lastly, each objective must have a measure and a criteria for passing as well as a specified evaluator and setting for evaluation (75 percent on test to pass/teacher administers in classroom).

*Chapter Three*

# Collaborative Relationships

KEY POINTS

- Collaborative relationships
    o Must be meaningful and goal-oriented
    o Must be connected to a mission objective
    - Keeps collaborations focused
    - Binds parties in collaborations through
    - Shared responsibility
    - Each person has a job in the collaboration
    - Shared decision making
    - Opportunity to identify and solve problems
- Student collaborations
    o Benefits of collaborations with adults
    - Develops decision-making skills
    - Fosters cooperation between students and teachers
- Staff collaborations
    o Assign roles
    - List each role in the collaboration along with responsibilities
- Set up protocol for decision making
    o List problems that they can and cannot solve
    o List predefined solutions that collaborations may use
    o Designate a staff or leader to have veto power

Building a cooperative environment incorporates all parties with a connection to the school supporting and engaging in the daily activities of the school. This includes forming collaborative relationships among students, teachers, leadership, counselors, librarians, on-site social workers, school psychologists, parents, and the community. (Please see table 3.1). The relationships must be meaningful to all parties involved and goal-oriented.

Think about this scenario. One of the objectives in a particular school includes increasing the oral reading fluency of fourth graders. As part of achieving this goal, the school hosted a program where volunteers read and listened to fourth graders read for thirty minutes three days a week. This collaborative relationship between the student and the volunteer allows the student to work on fluency while giving the volunteer a chance to contribute to the literacy program at the school.

Because collaborative relationships focus on common goals, the shared goals must precede forming the collaborative relationships in the form of mission objectives. As discussed in chapter two, creating mission objectives puts students and staff on the same page using the same vocabulary. This common intent binds the students, staff, administration, and volunteers together through shared responsibility and decision making.

Shared responsibility means each person does his or her part in order to achieve a common goal. Shared decision making entails each party having the opportunity to be a part of identifying and solving problems. Connecting collaborative relationships to mission objectives maintains focus on a shared mission. Making the connection among collaborative relationships and mission objectives also eliminates collaborative relationships that are not aligned with what the school wants to accomplish.

## STUDENT COLLABORATIONS

Students cooperate with peers in cooperative learning, but children also need to be a part of a school environment that allows students to collaborate with staff and volunteers. Team configurations that consist of students and adults in a school building help kids to develop decision-making skills. They also foster a sense of cooperation between students and adults within a school.

When adults value student input, students feel safe enough to share their opinions and thoughts. Having collaborative relationships between students and adults shows students that adults care about what they have to say. Studies show that this is important for children and adults.

Student/adult configurations come in many forms including, but not limited to, student council, yearbook, mediation committees, governance boards, portfolio development, event-planning committees, student-led parent conferences, and student-conducted school meetings. See table 3.1.

Table 3.1

Examples of Collaborative Relationships

| | |
|---|---|
| *Lein et al., 1997; Keyes & Udvari-Solner, 1999; Trimble, 2002; Picucci et al, 2010* | Team problem solving (including identification of problems), student-conducted school meetings, mediation committee consisting of students and one counselor, licensed clinical social worker (LCSW) on-site |
| *Griffith, 2003; Hair, Kraft, & Allen, 2001; Thiessen & Anderson, 1999; Sanders, 2010* | Between students and teachers, teachers and parents, principals and teachers as well as communication among teachers |
| *Hair, Kraft, & Allen, 2001; Sanders, 2010* | Teachers work in grade levels to examine student work and discuss ways to modify instruction to better meet student needs |
| *Trimble, 2002; Hair, Kraft, & Allen, 2001; Sanders, 2010* | Interdisciplinary teams, administrative teams, grade level teams, school improvement teams, content area teams, student support teams, and special focus teams |
| *Jones & Ross, 1994; Shields et al., 1995; Lein et al., 1997; Corallo & McDonald, 2001; Glickman, 2002; Craig, et al., 2005; Sanders, 2010* | Governance structure, shared decision making, team conferences, weekly student check-ups, portfolio development, students create own schedule, students suggest courses that teachers teach |

Consider the following example of how one school collaborates among students and teachers. Once a week, a school meeting occurs to identify and resolve issues. Students preside over the meeting. Students and teachers vote on issues after a discussion. Each person present gets one vote. Teacher and student votes carry the same weight. Decisions made in the school meeting become official school decisions. Every person, including students, is invested in the process.

Teachers give up a great deal of the decision-making power in the name of democracy, but educators also gain the satisfaction of knowing that the process actively teaches what a democracy looks like as well as how to develop decision-making skills.

## STAFF COLLABORATIONS

Staff collaborations range from cooperative relationships with students to collaborative relationships with community members. The foundation for collaborative relationships at any educational institution hinges on staff collaborations. Leadership and licensed staff should collaborate to set up protocols for all collaborative relationships within the building.

Once adults set specific rules and guidelines that establish procedure, collaborative relationships can effectively proceed. Then, all stakeholders can execute the mission objectives connected to collaborative relationships.

According to research, shared decision making proves to be an imperative component of high-performing schools. Because decisions affect more than leadership, it is vital that other school participants who are affected by school-wide decisions help in the decision-making process. When staff participates in the process, the shared leadership can create buy-in and show that staff opinions matter to leadership.

It is not enough to have a shared vision. The school staff must be a part of developing and achieving the vision as well as identifying/resolving issues pertaining to the vision. The leadership team (leader and staff members) takes the responsibility of ensuring that collaborative relationships perform the tasks germane to the collaboration. This can mean that one PLC (professional learning community) takes on the responsibility for a particular collaboration while another PLC sets up a different collaboration. For instance, the seventh-grade language arts teachers within a building might set up and run the collaborative relationships between peer tutors and tier-three Response to Intervention (RTI) students. Likewise, grade-level PLCs within the same building may establish guidelines for how student-led parent conferences are run.

Ultimately, the leadership team sets the boundaries for collaborative relationships. Every person, including students, volunteers, staff members, and leaders agree to abide by established boundaries. Look at the following steps to see how collaborative relationships can be set up to provide a school team with the tools it needs to carry out the mission objectives of the school.

### Step One: Assign Roles

Assigning roles helps students know what is expected of them. Once roles are identified, tasks associated with the particular role can be focused on. Designating roles adds clarity to cooperative relationships while avoiding conflict over who does which job.

The leadership team ultimately assigns a designator or designates which collaborative relationships should be formed. Once formed, the team of adults in charge holds the responsibility of assuring that students/volunteers know which job they are to do and what each role entails including limitations placed on their roles. Collaborative relationships operate effectively when the roles and tasks associated with the roles are identified beforehand.

Assigning positions enhances the collaboration process. Because many of the collaborations consist of students and unlicensed staff or volunteers, assigning roles is crucial. Students, adult volunteers and other unlicensed staff need guidance in how to effectively contribute to the education process. Remember that students and volunteers are not licensed education professionals. This means that they lack essential educational expertise that leadership and licensed educators possess.

Start by listing mission objectives to be supported by the collaborative relationship. What does the team hope to accomplish from the relationship? Make a list of the roles and the responsibilities for each role. Then, connect the mission objective to the collaborative relationship. Consider how the following example connects the collaborative relationship to the school's mission objective through its evidence.

## *Mission Objective Supported by Collaborative Relationship*

One hundred percent of students attending will serve in different capacities on an ongoing basis as part of our school community's democratic society as evidenced by the school's student-conducted weekly meetings (collaborative relationship).

A properly constructed mission objective leads a school to collaborative relationships that support the objective. In the case above, the collaborative relationship serves as the actual evidence (school's student-conducted weekly meetings) that proves the mission objective is being accomplished. Take the time to review the following roles and responsibilities students and teachers had in the student-conducted weekly meetings. See table 3.2.

Other relationships can be formed using the same objective with different evidence that spells out a different collaborative relationship. Reflect on the same mission objective with different evidence.

## *Mission Objective with Different Evidence*

One hundred percent of students attending will serve in different capacities on an ongoing basis as part of our school community's democratic society as evidenced by the school's election and service of school officers.

Notice that the mission objective is the same, but the evidence that the objective is being accomplished is different.

*Ban*: discussing or voting on curriculum/academic matters, staff development, certain discipline issues, security, or health matters.

Table 3.2 Student-conducted weekly meetings

| Roles | Responsibilities |
|---|---|
| Student | Attend meetings, determine how the meeting would be set up, conduct the school meeting, discuss ideas/issues pertinent to school life, give attendees opportunity to discuss ideas/issues, vote on issues, and support decisions made through the democratic process |
| Teacher | Set the rules and limitations for the collaboration, attend meetings, vote on issues, and support decisions made through the democratic process |

Limitations must be established and spelled out to all parties involved. In this case, the limitations included a ban on discussing or voting on curriculum/academic matters, staff development, certain discipline issues, security, or health matters. These matters lend themselves solely to adult collaborations. Both students and teachers must know their roles and responsibilities before the collaboration becomes an important aspect of the school environment. (Please see table 3.2.)

## Step Two: Set Up Protocol for Decision Making

Once roles have been assigned and each person understands what their responsibilities are, then the rules of engagement must be established. The essence of setting up protocols for decision making lies in establishing guidelines for collaborative relationships so everyone involved can identify and/or resolve problems without creating more issues. This becomes another responsibility for the leadership team.

First, the leadership team makes a list of the type of problems the collaboration is allowed to solve as well as the kind of dilemmas each cooperative is not allowed to resolve. It will depend on the type of collaboration and how much latitude the administrator and staff want to allow. A school team may want to specify which issues the collaborative team is free to resolve, leaving out those dilemmas they are not permitted to tackle.

Think about the following guidelines for a mediation committee consisting of students and one counselor. The mediation committee resolves only issues between students in the following designated areas:

- Recess disputes not involving weapons, drugs, injury/threats, or academic issues
- Classroom issues not involving weapons, drugs, injury/threats, or academic issues
- Afterschool dilemmas not involving weapons, drugs, injury/threats, or academics
- Bathroom issues not involving weapons, drugs, injury/threats, or academic issues

*Note: The counselor will have total veto power in the case of inappropriate decisions. (This should be predefined).*

In this case where a team decides to employ a mediation team as in the above example, it would be important to create a list of solutions that students can choose from instead of keeping it open-ended. Peruse the list of predefined approved solutions for the mediation committee.

- Serve afterschool detention
- Suspend from sports team for a period of time (one day to one week)
- Memorize the school rules and recite to the committee or designated person
- Apologize, agree not to name-call or disrespect
- Conduct student run trial/suspension if found guilty (two days to one week)
- Write essay explaining why infraction was inappropriate and list alternative ways problems could have been handled
- Suspend from all afterschool activities (per activity schedule)
- Take field trip privileges away (per semester or grading period)
- Suspend: In-school suspension
- Do clean-up duty after school and during free time at school (up to thirty days)

Protocols remain a valuable asset in providing a guideline for collaborative relationships, especially student collaborations. While it is important to allow students the chance to be a part of collaborations, it is equally vital to understand that improper protocols can create issues that tear at the very fabric of collaborative relationships often ruining the possibilities.

Take the time to think through collaborative relationships, especially those involving students and nonstaff. Always have a staff member or leader on the team who has veto power in case of inappropriate decisions. Make it clear to all collaborations that this is how it works so no one will be surprised, and everything will run smoothly.

The added protection does not ever have to be utilized, but it is extremely wise to have the option for everyone's protection. Certain types of responsibilities should never be put on the shoulders of students, parents or community members. It is, after all, the educator's responsibility to shoulder certain responsibilities.

## CHAPTER SUMMARY

Forming collaborative relationships as part of a cooperative environment should feature configurations among administration, staff, students, and community members. The interactions need to be meaningful. Each collaborative relationship should have a designated goal. This shared aspiration must be connected to a mission objective. Making the connection not only keeps collaborative relationships focused, but it also exposes any relationships that do not line up with what the school wants to accomplish.

The mission objective binds parties in collaborative relationships together through shared responsibility and decision making. Shared responsibility means each person has a job to do in the relationship. Collective decision making incorporates parties having the chance to identify issues as well as resolve problems.

Student collaborations are important. Configurations that allow students to collaborate with staff and volunteers are equally significant. Student/adult configurations offer two essential benefits: develop decision-making skills in students, and encourage a sense of cooperation between students and adults in a school building. Additionally, student collaborations show that adults in a school building respect the opinions of students.

Student/adult configurations might include: student council, yearbook, mediation committee, governance boards, portfolio development, event-planning committees, student-led parent conferences, and student-conducted school meetings.

Prior to any collaborative relationship forming, leadership and staff set up protocols for operating. These protocols serve as guidelines and rules that establish procedure for all collaborations in a school building. When done properly, stakeholders can effectively achieve the mission objective connected to the collaborative relationship. It is ultimately the staff's responsibility to oversee the relationship and put boundaries in place that all participants agree to abide by.

First, staff members assign roles to each participant. This means each party in the collaborative relationship will have a designated role with spelled-out responsibilities. (See table 3.2.) It is important that each party understand what they are responsible for doing. This will ultimately eliminate a lot of confusion about who does what. Equally important to collaborations is the placement of limitations on each relationship. In other words, staff must also state what parties in the collaboration are not allowed to do. (See *Ban* under table 3.2.)

The last step that the leadership team must accomplish is the setting up of protocols for decision making. Designated relationships will need to be free to identify and/or resolve problems without creating more issues. As such, it is wise for staff to create a list of predefined issues that collaborations are allowed to solve as well as those that are off limits.

Also, the leadership team should make an approved list of solutions that participants can choose from in solving dilemmas. As added protection, all collaborations with students and nonstaff should stipulate that a designated staff member or leader will have veto power. Be upfront and let all collaborators know the rules of engagement from the start, and everything will likely run smoothly. Planning will be the key to success.

*Chapter Four*

# Family/School/Community Connections

KEY POINTS

Family/school/community connections

- Must be meaningful
- The benefits
    o Students achieve more
    o Families respect school employees more
    o Community members tend to support school efforts more
- Executing a plan
    o Form a planning team especially for getting volunteers
    o Follow the two-step process
    - List volunteer opportunities
    • Make information sheets for each volunteer opportunity
    • Do background checks before offering volunteer opportunities
    - Formally invite families and community members to volunteer
    • Host a volunteer fair to present opportunities
    • Host a conference to recruit stakeholders

When schools discover ways to connect to families and communities, everyone involved benefits from the collaboration. Students tend to achieve more, family members often respect school employees more, and community members support school efforts more. Of course, these connections must be real, not contrived. Busywork for family and community members is not good enough. Parents and community members need to know that they are contributing to the process of schooling in a meaningful way.

Connecting to the community and families comes in many forms. It can be as simplistic as asking a parent to volunteer in a class or as complex as incorporating different cultures across the curriculum. See Table 4.1.

There are essentially two steps a school team can follow to execute family/school/community connections. The first step in the process prepares the school team for the second step. The school team will want to make a list of all the volunteer opportunities that are available to family and community members. This preparation step entails doing the legwork to guarantee that families and community members are eligible to volunteer. Once, the preparatory foundation has been laid, the team is now ready to formally extend the invitation to family and community members to volunteer.

## Step One: Get Clearance/List Opportunities

Having a list of opportunities readily available gives family and community members a chance to choose how they want to contribute to the school. Make sure the list has variety, something for those who work during the day and those who don't. Remember to leave room for opportunities that family or community members may suggest. More is better in this case.

Table 4.1

Examples of Family/School/Community Connections

| | |
|---|---|
| *Simons and Curtis, 2007; Sanders, 2010* | Share space, recruit volunteers, incorporate traditions for families and community members |
| *Griffith, 1999; Sanders, 2010* | Students felt safe, cared about by teachers and, thus, were able to meet academic standards; teachers and parents felt principals were available with necessary resources and to hear concerns; parents and teachers indicated that principals cared about their well-being and gave them a chance to contribute to the school |
| *Newmann & Wehlage, 1995; Cotton, 2000; Henderson & Mapp, 2002; Griffith, 2003; Daggett, 2005; Sanders, 2010* | Families and community members were given the opportunity to be a part of the school's activities, planning, and achievement of goals made a positive impression on students |
| *North Central Regional Educational Laboratory (NCREL), 2004; Sanders, 2010* | Family-like atmosphere contributed directly to student achievement; strong sense of community shared by students, parents, teachers, and administrators; shared vision and a sense of belonging to something special and unique |

Some projects may potentially be done solely by parents with a faculty member as a check-in person. Typically, parents and community members understand that volunteer opportunities that include working with children or around children will require some type of legal background check. It is wise to have family and community members fill out the paper work for this before actual sign-up opportunities are presented.

Even family members who do not wish to volunteer can be routinely asked to fill out the clearance papers so the clearance can be on file in the event the person decides to volunteer later. Be patient and wait for clearance before moving on to step two. This will save staff and families a great deal of time and anguish. Peruse the list The Academy made for volunteer opportunities available to family and community members.

- classrooms, sports activities, seasonal/holiday events, fundraising efforts
- school planning committee, PTA, school governance committee, creating media
- creating, updating or maintaining school website, attendance office, main office
- bus duty, afterschool patrol, career exploration planning committee, class speaker
- setting up or maintaining online communication system between parents and staff
- "Fridays in Session" committee, career mentor, community service provider
- hallway monitor, workshop/seminar presenter, tutoring, reading partner
- host internship, oversee service learning project
- set up/oversee telephone system that checks on student progress
- suggestions:
  _____
  _____

The list can be as long or as short as preferred. Be creative. Make an information sheet for each volunteer opportunity explaining the procedure for volunteering and the guidelines for serving in that particular volunteer capacity. This may seem like a great deal of work, but in the long run, it will pay off.

Preparation positions the school team to connect family and community members to the school. Notice that the above list has quite a few opportunities that do not include working with children, or in classrooms, or at the school. Try to cover as many bases as possible.

The same information sheets can be utilized every year, revamping as needed. As discussed in chapter three, spelling out the guidelines will pay off when issues arise. This type of structure is expected and respected in a school environment.

## Step Two: Extend an Invitation

The process of connecting with parents and community members carries an inevitable opportunity to extend an invitation to those who the team would like to contribute to the process of schooling or be a part of the process in some meaningful manner.

In other words, efforts should be made to connect to as many family members as possible and get the support of the community. This is where staff should take the time to be different and creative. Make a big deal out of volunteering. If it seems important to staff and leadership, it will become important to family and community members. They will take the lead from leadership and staff.

Have an open house to present volunteer opportunities. Host a conference where staff recruits school helpers. This conference can have booths featuring volunteer opportunities. Have a "by invitation only" meeting to solicit volunteers. Use these events to present the opportunity list, introduce information sheets, present speeches about being a part of the school's vision, and ask for other ideas about volunteer opportunities. These practical ideas help to make volunteering a priority in the minds of potential volunteers.

Regardless of the avenue taken, make the invitations fancy. Ask parents and community members to RSVP. For households that don't reserve their places, make it a priority to contact a family member via telephone or house visit to let them know that their potential contribution does count.

If they are unable to come to the event, set up a personal meeting to talk about the volunteer options. If work conflicts with the parent's work hours, point out some of the volunteer opportunities that will allow the parent to contribute to the school without being at school or a school event.

Maybe a parent would be willing to do a fundraiser at his job to help kids who cannot afford to participate in sports, or maybe the parent's job would be willing to sponsor a walk to raise money for physical education uniforms.

Think involvement. What would or could the person do to be a part of the school? Stress the significance of family members being a part of the school team. Read the following execution plan:

1. Hold a school campaign to get parents and community members to fill out clearance forms to work with or around students. Take the forms to businesses in the community and post on community bulletin boards for community members.
2. In the meantime, leadership and staff can work on the information sheets for volunteer opportunities while waiting for forms to come in and potential volunteers to be cleared. Assign information sheets to different staff members.

3. The school does an invitation-only conference inviting potential parent and community volunteers.

Try forming a committee to work specifically on the campaign to get family and community members to fill out and turn in clearance forms. A separate PLC can work on the volunteer information sheets. Still another group can work out the details of the volunteer conference.

## CHAPTER SUMMARY

Authentic connections to families and communities lead to improved student achievement. In this type of cooperative environment, families respect school employees more, and community members tend to support school efforts more. When schools connect to families and communities, all stakeholders have the opportunity to contribute to the process of schooling in a meaningful way.

A school team can follow two relevant steps in order to connect stakeholders to a school. First, the leadership team should create a list of volunteer opportunities for family and community members. It is wise to also develop an information sheet for each volunteer opportunity. The information sheet should explain the how-to of volunteering and lay out the guidelines and rules for serving in each volunteer capacity.

Before proceeding to step two, make sure that stakeholders can get clearance to volunteer. Have potential volunteers fill out forms for a background check which will be required for volunteers in any school. The school team will need to be creative in step two. Extend a formal invitation to potential volunteers. Host a volunteer fair to present opportunities or a conference to recruit stakeholders. Create a special team to execute the above steps. The hard work will be well worth the effort.

# II

# Accountability — The A in the CAB Model

Accountability is the backbone of a cooperative school environment. As is consistent with cooperativeness, all parties in the school building have designated roles in an accountability system. Leadership sets up the accountability system, teachers manage the system so students can measure up to the expectations of the accountability system. Inherent in the system is the high expectations leadership, teachers, and students are subject to and work toward achieving in order to make the system work.

*Chapter Five*

# Staff Accountability

### KEY POINTS

- Accountability
    - o Leader
    - - Set up accountability system
    - - School-wide philosophy, mission/vision, mission objectives
    - - Monitor accountability system in a tone of high expectations
    - - Check school programs and curriculum
    - - Does it align with school-wide guiding philosophy?
    - - Does it line up with mission objectives?
    - - Align curriculum with state and national content standards
    - o Professional development
    - - Does it connect to classroom learning?
    - - Does it connect to a mission objective?
    - - Does it have a how-to component?
- Teachers
    - o Leading students to accountability
    - - Switch paradigms
    - - Take responsibility for student learning
    - - Set high standards
    - - Provide a means to meet standards through resources and services

Imagine receiving a huge gift box. Inside the box is another gift box. When the second gift box is opened, an even smaller gift box is inside of it. Accountability in schools compares perfectly to that huge gift box with a smaller box inside holding an even smaller box. Leadership accountability symbolizes that huge gift box, while teacher accountability represents the second gift box. Student accountability depicts the smallest gift box.

In schools, accountability starts with leadership. Leadership must set up an accountability system at the building level in order for all school participants, including teachers, and students to be held accountable in the same manner. This is all part of building a cooperative environment which is the foundation of a true CAB school.

If the school-level administrator fails to set up an accountability system, staff members will not be able to adequately perform their job duties and be held accountable on the same terms. As a result, students will not rise up to high expectations or even mediocre expectations.

When an effective accountability system prevails, it gives teachers the foundation to set up a consistent accountability system for students. The accountability system does need to be top-down. If the accountability system is not top-down, teachers will be forced to incorporate a variety of accountability systems for students.

Teachers understand that there has to be some type of checks and balances system for students. The inconsistencies that will surface in a variety of noncooperative accountability systems work against efforts to produce a cooperative school environment.

Staff members need to be on the same page when it comes to executing an accountability system, or it will not work. Students will not respond to accountability systems holding some students accountable in one way, while holding other students accountable in another way. This will inevitably lead to having a deluge of disgruntled students with feelings of being treated unfairly. Whether students fail or succeed in school, pupils share one commonality: All learners want to be treated with equity and held to the same level of accountability.

## LEADERSHIP

Let's unpack that huge gift box we mentioned earlier in this chapter by considering what a leader has the responsibility of doing in terms of accountability. A leader's first task includes setting up an accountability system in a tone of high expectations.

The leader himself must be the first to meet high expectations that produce results in terms of school improvement and high student achievement. Not only does the leader set up an accountability system, but the school-level administrator must also be skilled at maintaining an efficient accountability system. This is the first of three steps in leadership accountability.

The second step in the process includes aligning curriculum with state and national content standards. Once the second stage of leadership accountability passes the alignment test, the third stage of leadership accountability will be a natural progression. This last stage in leadership accountability requires that the leader ensures that professional development connects to classroom learning.

## Step One: Set Up/Monitor Accountability System

The good news for leaders in setting up an accountability system is that if the leader or team went through the process in chapter two of developing a school-wide guiding philosophy through the creation of vision and mission statements as well as mission objectives, a viable accountability system has already been set up along with expectations included.

In this case, it will be a matter of monitoring the system against school programs. Do the school's programs line up with the school-wide guiding philosophy and mission objectives? How about the curriculum? Does it line up with the school-wide guiding philosophy and mission objectives? Everything in the school should line up with the school-wide guiding philosophy and mission objectives.

Monitor each program to see if it is accomplishing what the team wants to accomplish in terms of the school's mission objectives. It is equally important to make sure that programs or curriculum do not in any way violate the school-wide guiding philosophy.

Any programs or curriculum that does not help accomplish what the school team has set out to achieve on a daily basis should be eliminated or revamped until it is in line with what the school stands for and what the school team wants to achieve. Consider how a school leader checked the school's programs against the school-wide guiding philosophy and mission objectives in table 5.1.

Be sure to give the school team the time to accomplish the mission objective. Look at the first mission objective again: One hundred percent of students attending The Academy will perform at grade level in all subjects comparable to peers throughout the world within three years of attending The Academy as indicated by teachers surveying student portfolio records at the end of each semester and comparing to peer groups.

Note that the school has three years to meet the objective. If the requirements have not been met in the allotted time, revamp the program with specific changes to help the school meet the objectives. The answers should be: yes (Y), which means good job, No (N), which means eliminate the program or Revamp to meet (R), which means change the program.

Table 5.1

| Programs | School-Wide Guiding Philosophy: Is the program in line with what we stand for? | Mission Objectives: Is the program in line with what we want to accomplish? |
|---|---|---|
| Fridays-in-Session | Y | Y |
| Career Exploration | Y | Y |
| Community Service | Y | Y |
| Character Education | Y | Y |
| Technology Program | Y | Y |
| Grade-Level Expectations | Y | Y-allotted time has not passed |
| Standardized Testing Expectations | Y | R |
| Curriculum | Y | Y |

Note that some of the programs may be in line with what the school wants to achieve even though it has not reached a point of actual fulfillment yet. State this fact on the table as shown in table 5.1 (allotted time has not passed).

## Step Two: Align Curriculum with Standards

After completing the curriculum checklist done in the prior step to see if curriculum lines up with what the school stands for and what the team wants to accomplish, the team is ready to check whether curriculum aligns with state and national content standards. It is crucial to test curriculum against both state and national standards so the school will have the highest standards possible. Though a leader may assign this task to others, it is the leader's responsibility to make sure that this task is done thoroughly and completely.

Don't make any assumptions. Meeting national content standards does not automatically mean that the school meets state standards or visa versa. A table much like table 5.1 can be used. Of course, the school team or leader will need to have state and national standards on hand to complete this exercise. Use the following table (table 5.2) as a guide in making a template for the school team.

Answers will be: meets standards (M), which means the curriculum meets all the standards in that subject area or did not meet standards (D), which means curriculum did not meet all the standards in that subject area. If the answer is *D*, specify the exact content standard that curriculum did not meet.

The school team will need to decide on whether to adopt a new curriculum which has all the content standards or buy supplementary materials in that subject area that meet the standards that have not been met by the main curriculum in that subject area. The school team will probably choose the latter unless the main curriculum is substantially missing content standards in a particular subject.

The leadership team should do a check anytime new curriculum is considered. Some suppliers of textbooks may have already linked standards to the curriculum. Seek out these suppliers. It can save a great deal of time.

## Step Three: Connect Staff Development to Classroom Learning

The key to this step lies in making professional development practical. It is not enough to require staff to get in a predetermined amount of staff development hours. Those professional development hours must connect to classroom learning.

Additionally, the staff development must be practical in nature, as opposed to theoretical. In other words, the class, workshop, seminar, or even book must have a how-to component as part of the instruction.

Table 5.2

| *Curriculum* | *State Content Standards* | *National Content Standards* |
|---|---|---|
| *Mathematics* | | |
| *Language Arts* | | |
| *Science* | | |
| *Social Sciences* | | |
| *The Arts* | | |
| *Foreign Language* | | |
| *Physical Education* | | |
| *Health Education* | | |
| *Technology* | | |

It is important to align professional development with the mission objectives in order to ensure that staff development is practical for teachers and in line with what the school endeavors to accomplish on a daily basis.

Research! Opportunities can come in any form. Leadership and/or staff may offer a mandatory service learning day which consists of brainstorming sessions on how to connect a particular mission objective to a subject area. Another professional development day may be used by staff to study a book that shows how to implement one of the mission objectives in the classroom.

Provide staff with an approved list of professional development opportunities. Make sure to highlight which teachers the staff development opportunity is applicable to. The list of approved opportunities should be updated at the beginning of each semester, at the very least.

Ask for suggestions from staff members for staff development opportunities that meet the requirements of aligning professional development with a mission objective and ensuring that the staff development has a how-to component. Peruse the examples which match professional development opportunities to mission objectives in table 5.3.

Note that these are just ideas for the types of staff development opportunities a leadership team might be searching for and conducting, as well as looking for professionals with the expertise to present on these topics. Notice that they are all derived from the mission objectives.

## TEACHERS

Like everything else, teacher accountability has a bottom line. That bottom line involves the teacher's willingness. Exactly what is the teaching staff willing to do to get results? Will teachers do whatever it takes for students to learn? Are they really willing to think outside the box or are they set on doing what they have always done? And most importantly, will teachers do their part in the accountability cycle?

These are important questions for a leader and teachers to answer together. An administrator can establish the best accountability system in the world, but teachers must be willing to make it happen within the predefined parameters or it will prove to be futile. Like leadership accountability, teacher accountability proves to be crucial to the process that leads to student accountability.

Unfortunately, there is no way to measure whether a teacher has a willing heart. A leader can only take the teacher's word for whether the professional is willing or not. However, an administrator can watch for signs that some teachers may not be willing to execute the predetermined accountability system. This will become apparent as staff participates in shared leadership.

Table 5.3

| Mission Objectives | Professional Development Opportunities |
|---|---|
| 11 | International chat to solve math problems in the classroom—*math and foreign language teachers* |
| 1, 2, 11 | Project co-ops with international students—*math and science teachers* |
| 1, 2, 11 | Problem-solving exchange with foreign students—*math and foreign language teachers* |
| 10 | Adding a research component to lessons |
| 8 | How to use software fluency tests to boost software fluency |
| 9 | Increasing computer hardware knowledge in students |
| 11 | Teaching students to thrive in computer-based learning environments |
| 7 | Lessons that increase World Wide Web capabilities |
| 8 | Increasing software fluency in students |
| 6 | Incorporating democratic model into a school environment—*social studies teachers* |
| 7, 8, 9, 10, 11 | How students can measure up to technology demands in the 21st century |
| 10 | Testing research knowledge |
| 5 | Building character through lessons |
| 1, 2 | Global debating competitions for students—*language arts teachers* |
| 1, 2 | Global science fair opportunities for students—*science teachers* |
| 1, 2, 7, 8, 9 | Preparing students for a global marketplace |
| 1, 2 | Preparing students to meet national standards |
| 4, 5 | Community service opportunities that build character—*social studies teachers* |
| 3 | Tying math lessons to careers—*math teachers* |
| 1, 2, 3 | Competing with Japanese students in mathematics—*math teachers* |

While a leader may not be able to make a teacher have a willing heart, a leader can motivate and encourage teachers to execute the accountability system.

There are three steps that will assist teachers in leading students to accountability: switching paradigms, setting high standards, and providing a means to meet standards. It will become evident that these three steps have an inherent checks-and-balances system.

The first step is contingent upon the second step and the second step depends on the third step. Switching paradigms prevents teachers from limiting students to low expectations, while committing to hold students to high expectations encourages teachers to provide services and resources that challenge students to meet those high expectations.

## Step One: Switch Paradigms

It is easy to fall into the "I have done everything I can do" trap. This mindset is also dangerous to the ultimate goal of student learning. If educators think this way, then there is nothing else that can be done to change low performance in schools. The responsibility is no longer personal. It becomes the student's responsibility to try harder or be more motivated. After all, the teacher has done his part. It is time for students to do their part. Right?

This attitude encourages teachers to keep doing what has always been done, hoping that students will eventually rise up. This is no longer an option for teachers.

Accountability laws like No Child Left Behind (NCLB) basically says that it is the teacher who must rise up to the challenge of structuring school in a manner that encourages students to learn. The burden is no longer on the student. It is now on the teacher. The teacher carries the golden egg: Expertise wrapped in knowledge. Expertise along with teaching skill is why teachers are hired.

It pays to come up with a one-sentence slogan that reminds teachers that all students have learning potential and teachers have the daily task of tapping into student potential. The slogan should clearly declare the mindset teachers in the building have toward the child's potential to learn and the teacher's willingness to tap into that potential.

Keep it short and simple. Say the slogan at the beginning of every staff meeting. Place it in a prominent place in every classroom. Put the slogan in the hallways. Posting the slogan will help the school team change its attitude, let students know staff believes in them, and remind parents how committed to their children the school team is.

Consider some examples of one sentence slogans that may help staff members have a change in attitude. These slogans were paraphrased from attitude changes reported in different studies. The attitude changes were instrumental in school change.

- We believe all students can learn (Shields et al, 1995; TEA, 2000).
- We will teach students until they get it because we know they are capable (Kannapel et al, 2005).
- We change our strategies to fit our students (Daggett, 2005; Craig et al, 2005).

- We teach so students learn; re-teach so student retain, and test so students can think (TEA, 2000; Reeves, 2005).
- Failure brings us one step closer to success because we choose to learn from it (Lein et al, 1997; Reeves, 2005).
- Every student will meet district, state, and national content standards (USDE, 1999; Hair et al, 2001; Billig et al, 2005).

Be clear in slogans and make sure the slogan is specific to the attitude change that needs to happen within the school building.

## Step Two: Set High Standards

Once the team comes up with a slogan to remind the school team of its commitment to students, it will be easy to set high standards for students. Educators know that all kids deserve the best education. The school team would have proven that they are now determined to give students the best by setting high expectations.

It is perfectly acceptable to admit that students will not be able to reach the high standards in the beginning. This is what teachers are for. Teachers will scaffold students until they are able to meet the high expectations. Splurge when setting standards. Do not skimp. Make expectations high in every subject area.

Do not just offer remedial classes to low-achieving students. Offer advanced placement (AP) and International Baccalaureate (IB) classes to failing students. The importance of setting high standards for every student prevails in the attitude of students. Low-achieving students want to be offered the same opportunities as high-achieving students.

It can make students feel valued and that they are being treated fairly. Ultimately, all students want teachers to have confidence in them. Students expect teachers to help them become high-achieving students against all odds. Failure becomes positive when it is used as a learning tool to scaffold students to success. Think about some of the following ways other schools have set high expectations for students and staff.

- Scaffold students until kids take ownership of their own learning (Scribner & Scribner, 2001).
- School theme that concentrated efforts into the success of every student. Every aspect of schooling, including curriculum, programs, and school planning, focused on the success of every student (Edmonds, 1979; Newman & Wehlage, 1995; USDE, 1999; Hair et al, 2001; Reeves, 2005).
- Flexibility in changing teaching strategies until they work for the teacher and students. Changed attitude (Kannapel et al, 2005).

- Everyone is held accountable: leadership, teachers, and students (Shields et al, 1995; Keyes & Udvari-Solner, 1999; Scribner & Scribner, 2001; Picucci et al, 2002; Billig et al, 2005).
- All students can learn. Same expectations for all students (JLARC, 2003; Ellis et al, 2004; Billig et al, 2005).
- Eliminate all remedial classes (Billig et al, 2005).
- Link high expectations to district, state, and national content standards (Lockwood, 1996; WSDI, 2000; Craig et al, 2005; Billig et al, 2005; Daggett, 2005).
- Do whatever it takes for students to learn and meet high expectations (Lockwood, 1996; Picucci et al, 2002; Fouts, 2003; Billig et al, 2005).
- Attitude change from thinking that students need to help themselves to teachers realizing that they need to scaffold students to success (Connell, 1996).
- Professionalism: competence, concern for students, experience, commitment to student achievement, and effective teaching strategies (NCREL, 2004).

Notice that the slogans that remind staff to have a different attitude are similar to the slogans for setting high expectations. This is because having a more productive attitude will lead to setting high standards.

## Step Three: Provide Means to Meet Standards

Staff and leadership accountability! It is the responsibility of leadership and staff to not only set high expectations, but the school team must also provide the necessary services and resources in and out of class that will assist students in meeting the established high expectations. This means flexibility on the part of staff.

Teachers must be willing to experiment with different learning strategies and throw out any strategies that do not work for the student. This is where a teacher will need to remind herself that failure is part of the learning process for both teachers and students.

Outcome based education (OBE) can be utilized to scaffold students to student success. Through OBE and trying new strategies, teachers assess and reassess, teach and reteach as well as test and retest students. This becomes a part of the daily task of moving students toward meeting the high expectations that have been set.

Schools have done a variety of things to ensure student success. Reflect on how these schools did whatever it took to help students and staff meets high expectations:

- Looked at student weaknesses in terms of classroom and standardized test scores and tailored instruction to deal with the weakness. Referred students to tutoring (Billig et al, 2005).
- Made learning fun for kids. Concentrated on teaching kids to think rather than to memorize (Shields et al, 1995).
- Allowed students to take food home for supper or called to wake students up when parents were working (Lein et al, 1997).
- Offered tutoring, showed students how to study, included one on one instruction and offered programs to increase reading and math fluency (TEA, 2000; JLARC, 2003, Billig et al, 2005).
- The principal took teachers on field trips to local low and high-performing schools to compare the elements that determined success versus failure. He gave staff a tour of the surrounding neighborhoods so teachers could see firsthand how the children lived and what students dealt with outside of school. The same principal had staff read a book about poverty that they studied together with the principal as the facilitator (Hair et al, 2001).
- Leadership and staff studied several successful programs and worked hard to incorporate the programs at their school (Hair et al, 2001).
- Conducted a study of staff for a year that assigned, to a different grade level every month, the task of visiting different classrooms to learn about strategies that were working in the classroom. Staff collaborated on the results (Hair et al, 2001).

## INTERVIEW EXCERPT FROM AN ADMINISTRATOR

*If you can quantify it by the number of hours that a person is teaching or the number of students that a person is teaching, the levels at which the kids are achieving and that gets reviewed by student portfolio work which we all review because each student creates a portfolio of their work. So there's a piece to the conversation where we are all a part of kids developing portfolios.*

*So, we all need to present them with opportunities to do really rigorous work and if somebody is not doing that: "Yo (name of teacher) where's the Spanish stuff? Is there something happening? You doing that soon or what?" So, there is a very real conversation about what assignments are being given, what work is being done.*

*The expectation is that all teachers are prepping kids for college. Not all of our kids are going to college, but the piece is that all kids at the end of their senior year will be prepared for that. And, keeping the teachers abreast of what that means is my job and I keep up on that and Jenny helps with this too: for college placement offices, finding out what they need, and how are the expectations changing, all that.* (Sanders, 2009)

## CHAPTER SUMMARY

Setting up an accountability system is crucial for every school. The leader has the chore of being responsible for setting up and maintaining an accountability system. Before teachers can hold students accountable, teachers need to be held accountable. This accountability can only happen when leaders, teachers and students are held to the same standards in a tone of high expectations.

If a system is not top-down, each teacher will end up setting up accountability systems for students. These systems will not be consistent with one another. One student will be held accountable in one way while another will be held accountable in another way. Students will inevitably complain of unfairness. The lack of an effective accountability system tears at the very fiber of a cooperative environment.

Going through the process of developing a school-wide guiding philosophy, mission and vision statements as well as the mission objectives in chapter two will yield an effective accountability system. The next step is to monitor the system by checking to see if school programs and curriculum line up with the school-wide guiding philosophy and mission objectives.

The leader must also make sure that curriculum aligns with state and national content standards so the school can have the highest standards possible. Lastly, the administrator has the responsibility of ensuring that staff development is connected to classroom learning and the mission objectives. The professional development should also have a how-to component as part of the training.

Teachers also have a role in the accountability system. There are three steps that will assist teachers in leading students to accountability: switching paradigms (have an attitude that takes responsibility for student learning), setting high standards, and providing a means to meet standards (provide resources and services). These steps have an inherent checks-and-balances system.

*III*

# Boundlessness — The B in the CAB Model

A cooperative environment in which leadership, staff, and students are held accountable would not be complete without maintaining the characteristics of boundlessness. Boundlessness maintains an atmosphere of growth and consumption of knowledge that is practiced school-wide. Within this setting, leadership, staff, and students develop into school participants who are willing to be continuously evaluated so the highest level of student achievement can be realized. Being in this mode of continuous learning and growing requires a commitment to data-driven evaluation.

*Chapter Six*

# Data-driven School-wide Evaluation

KEY POINTS

**Boundlessness**

- Data-driven evaluation
    o Everyone has an attitude of continuous learning and growth
    o Evaluation is self-imposed
- Training staff to use data
    o Gather information
    - Consider relevant data
    o Analyze data
    - Conduct a needs assessment
    o Make data-driven decisions
- Train staff how to utilize data to inform
    - Professional development
    - Student achievement

Students learn. Teachers teach. Administrators lead. This epitomizes the typical expectation at schools throughout America. What is different about schools that practice boundlessness? In schools that practice boundlessness, everyone learns.

Schools operate in a mode of continuous growth and learning. In order to accomplish this task of perpetual advancement, schools utilize data to inform student achievement and staff development.

Decisions emerge out of careful analysis of relevant data. This analysis becomes part of the decision-making process. Constant self-imposed evaluation reflects a commitment to do the work that ultimately leads to school change. See table 6.1.

Essential to the concept of boundlessness is a school's propensity to train staff in how to use data-driven evaluation to make decisions that inform professional development and student achievement.

Read through the following excerpt of an interview with a school administrator and notice how they used data to evaluate and make decisions.

*The nature of our population is such that that is tough to really measure what we do. But, we do have a system called Measures of Academic Progress, MAPS, which is a testing system looking at reading, language arts, and math . . . It's a little better measure than the state online test called OAKS, and those are tied toward the CIM and the CAM. We do those as well, but we tend to see that the MAPS, Measures of Academic Progress, testing is one test-driven data that we can use to see where progress was.*

Table 6.1

Examples of Boundlessness

| | |
|---|---|
| USDE, 1999 | Assessment data, principal observations, or analyses of student work used to improve practice |
| Hair et al., 2001; Corallo and McDonald, 2001; Daggett 2005 | Linking student improvement to staff development |
| Reeves, 2005 | Data displayed in the form of graphs, tables, and charts in public places such as school offices and throughout the halls |
| Hair et al., 2001 | Analyze disaggregative test data in order to find areas of weakness for students across grade levels |
| Sanders, 2010 | Use of different types of data to improve practice: review of biweekly attendance data, weekly reporting of every student's progress, yearly review of program issues, cross-curricular review of particular areas, portfolio review in 8th, 11th, and 12th grades; MAPS & OAKS testing; student focus groups; parent surveys |
| Picucci et al., 2002; Lein et al., 1997 | Training staff how to use relevant data to improve student achievement and inform staff development |

> *Our big focus this year and next year, really ongoing, is on literacy because what we found is not really an earth shattering revelation, but that our kids need to be able to read effectively and be literate in order to succeed in other disciplines or subject areas. Because we have so many kids that are below grade level in reading, our focus is on, and even our fundraising efforts, is on providing resources for our kids to succeed and become successful readers . . . For the first time, we are developing actual libraries within our school. We're making a strong investment in individual tutoring. Our last one was just having cultural experiences that relate to literacy and art, things like that, so we're providing opportunities for that.*
>
> *That's (MAPS) like a test-driven data that we use and review annually. It allows us to do those pretests at the beginning of the year which helps us determine some of the classes kids should be in or groups they should be in.*
>
> *Just attendance data, the fact that a student has shown up here only 70 percent of the time when our goal is 90 percent attendance for all of our kids. That data there, we get weekly, daily, whatever. That's going to drive decisions on whether or not that student goes on an attendance contract, meaning they have to be in a certain attendance criteria in order to remain in the program and it could be over a 30-day period.*
>
> *The fact that we have a student that failed one or two classes during a quarter will drive the development of an academic contract for the following quarter and beyond. And that's in cooperation with the student and the parent because again, we are so small; and it's so geared toward being here and being successful that we look at each kid almost like an individual plan. That data drives that* (Sanders, 2009).

There are three basic steps a school takes to train staff in how to make decisions through data-driven evaluation. The first step involves gathering relevant data while the second stage depends on the analysis of the applicable data. In the last phase, the school makes a decision based on the evaluation of the data.

## Step One: Gather Relevant Information

By nature, schools perform formative and summative evaluations on a regular basis. Both forms of evaluation require data to achieve their purpose. The type of data collected will determine the quality of the end result.

Suppose The Academy's math department wants to adopt a new math curriculum. The math department would need to ask two essential questions: which mission objectives does the new math curriculum align with? And what predefined guidelines has the leader already set up in the school's accountability system that must be followed?

This is the data germane to the process that the math department will need to have on hand to make a decision that lines up with what the school seeks to accomplish. Consider the relevant data that The Academy would need to gather before starting the evaluation.

1. Mission objectives that the curriculum aligns with
2. State and national content standards

### Step Two: Analyze Relevant Data By Doing Needs Assessments

Once the team collects the relevant data, it is time to measure the data against the program or curriculum being evaluated. Look at the new math curriculum choices that the team is looking to adopt. Compare each curriculum to 1) the mission objectives that apply and 2) the district, state, and, national content standards. This will help us to narrow our curriculum choices down to the ones that specifically meet both our criteria.

Curriculum choices that do not measure up to the criteria will automatically be eliminated. The new curriculum choices will need to clearly help the school accomplish the relevant mission objectives as well as align with district, state, and, national content standards. This becomes the filter through which the needs assessment is passed.

The data must resolve the issue at hand. This is extremely important. The information gathered must be analyzed through a needs assessment, or the new curriculum or program will not resolve the issue.

### Step Three: Make a Decision

Now that the team carefully collected relevant data and evaluated the information against the potential curriculum by doing a need assessment, it is time to make a decision. The team can have confidence in the decision because the decision will line up with what the school wants to accomplish on a daily basis (mission objectives) and resolve the curriculum issue.

Additionally, the process of data-driven evaluation gives the institution an opportunity to act within the parameter of the accountability system which was set up to activate the high expectations for all school participants. Thus, the decision maintains the high expectations of the school.

## CHAPTER SUMMARY

Schools practicing boundlessness embrace continuous growing or learning. Everyone in the school operates in this mode. Self-evaluation is the norm. Decision comes out of gathering and looking at relevant data, analyzing the information through a needs assessment, and making an informed decision based on the analysis of data. Staff members are trained how to utilize data to inform student achievement and professional development.

The data-driven evaluation process allows a school to operate within the parameter of the accountability system. An effective accountability system activates high expectations in all school participants. As such, data-driven decision making perpetuates the goal of high expectations throughout the school.

*IV*

# The Inception of CAB

*Chapter Seven*

# The History of CAB

What is the practical answer to failing schools? How does research answer the question? This is how the doctoral dissertation topic began. The investigative journey to focus the topic proved to be an arduous task. Finding the key words to get the proper information took a great deal of time and effort. School improvement, school change, effective schools; all yielded data about schools, but not exactly a focus to the research.

Ultimately, the term *high performing schools* surfaced among studies. The studies on high performing schools yielded the type of insight that helped to focus the dissertation investigation. The search yielded answers to another set of relevant questions about school change.

What are high performing schools doing? How does a failing school become a high performing school? What characteristics do high performing schools have in common? After reviewing the literature on high performing schools, the answer to these new questions narrowed the focus of the research to one basic question: What characteristics do high performing schools have in common? Answering this question would at least indicate a commonality in successful schools and thus render some concept of the elements present in high performing schools.

In extracting the characteristics that are consistent in high performing schools, hundreds of studies on high performing schools were compared. Amazingly, the different traits found in high performing schools fall into similar themes. Three themes consistently surfaced: cooperativeness, accountability, and boundlessness. All of the characteristics were categorized under these three themes. Thus, the idea of the CAB model was born. Any school fully practicing all of the characteristics within the three themes are referred to as a CAB school.

# INTRODUCTION TO CAB RESEARCH

Case studies focusing on schools paint a picture about the daily activities, goals, and achievement within a school building. These studies usually reveal the true culture of the organization. In order to accomplish the task of truly understanding how a school functions, many case studies research specific characteristics of an institution.

Often, different schools are compared to discover if there are common traits within these education entities. Studies generally look at either high performing schools or low performing schools to get an idea about what can potentially contribute to a school being a high performing or low performing school.

CAB research concentrated its efforts on high performing schools. What characteristics do high performing schools have in common? And can these common traits help institutions perform at a higher level? Studies showed that successful schools do share some of the same traits. Furthermore, the characteristics that high performing schools possess can be utilized as a framework to help improve student achievement.

Communities no longer depend solely on school districts to help failing students. Many groups outside school districts form community-based education opportunities for students who do not measure up to the traditional school learning environment. Many districts partner with and encourage community groups who can meet the needs of students who thrive in a different type of school setting.

Community-based education opportunities have succeeded in increasing student performance at a portion of the cost to school districts. This has been especially true for minority and under-achieving students who tend to perform better in smaller school environments. The community-centered setting is now prevalent in community-based, alternative and traditional school settings. This concept of community-centered learning environment proves to be a vital element in the CAB model.

## CAB Research

For decades, two goals stood out in the efforts of educators and researchers: how to close the achievement gap and how to help failing students meet performance standards. In order to meet the challenge of these two goals, educators and researchers explored different avenues of school reform. How does the culture and structure of a school need to change to accomplish these goals? Research confirms that schools consistently meeting performance standards share some common characteristics which address this question.

School reform researchers first focused on the effective school models which addressed how schools function. The challenge of the effective school models included how to increase school effectiveness by improving student performance and how to utilize measures to monitor student progress. A popular model in 1963 was the Carroll Model.

The Carroll Model included four essential elements: Aptitude, perseverance, opportunity and quality of instruction. Aptitude is how much time it takes to learn a task under the best teaching condition and be able to comprehend the teaching. Perseverance is how much time the student puts forth effort to learn. Opportunity is the amount of time given to comprehend. Quality of instruction is an assessment of whether instruction accomplishes mastery within a reasonable amount of time given the student's aptitude.

Unfortunately, the Carroll Model was insufficient. It only concentrated on the student level of education leaving out other aspects of schooling. The Creemer Model focused on three additional focal points: classroom, school, and context levels. Other education models of the nineties endeavored to provide answers to education ills in a more comprehensive manner. None of the models were enough to capture the essence of school change. Children were still failing to meet performance standards and the achievement gap was widening.

In searching for approaches that worked, researchers bridged a marriage between school effectiveness and school improvement. The merging of both schools of thought was expected to yield more practical solutions. On the one hand, effectiveness research generally concentrates on restructuring schools in hopes of better student achievement. On the other hand, school improvement research focuses on school reformation through assessing and then revamping the cultural aspects of a school.

Measurable outcomes became the goal of the merger. Researchers wanted to see student achievement. Giving attention to more global designs yielded the realization that school improvement had to come through school effectiveness models. This means having benchmarks and standards that students must meet as an integral part of the reformation. It also meant restructuring in terms of the cultural elements of an institution of learning.

All-inclusive models surfaced as a result of merging the two schools of thought. Comprehensive education models shared some of the same characteristics as evidenced in high performing schools. There was finally a common ground. Educators and researchers could produce a framework utilizing mutual attributes. This framework itself would be an education model upon which schools could build. The education model born out of one of these communal frameworks is called CAB. CAB includes three themes: Cooperativeness, Accountability, and Boundlessness.

## CAB: COOPERATIVENESS

The first theme in the framework is cooperativeness. A CAB school operates in an atmosphere of cooperativeness. Everyone gets an opportunity to participate in making the school a place of high achievement. Teachers, principals, paraprofessionals, librarians, janitors, cooks, parents, students, and the community each fulfill a role in children meeting performance standards.

In cooperativeness, roles are not contrived. Each party in the network of participants understands community. To this end, cooperativeness consists of three concepts: school-wide guiding philosophy, collaborative relationships, and family/school/community connection.

### School-wide Guiding Philosophy

Because cooperativeness is contingent upon a network of people working toward the same goal, a school-wide guiding philosophy is essential. The school-wide guiding philosophy becomes the glue that keeps school staff, family, students, and the community working on one accord. It can be a document or a statement. A school-wide guiding philosophy can be a slogan, a mission statement, a list of rules, a statement of rights, a school plan, or a constitution.

This shared direction will by nature guide the daily happenings and operations of the school. As such, a shared philosophy is twofold, creating a sense of togetherness while keeping school participants focused on accomplishing the same task.

According to a study that focused on "Great Schools," a school-wide guiding philosophy should accomplish three things: be crafted in an environment of cooperativeness, specify how it looks when children are learning, as well as spell out what is expected of students. The researcher gives an example of how one school used its school-wide guiding philosophy to solve an issue with a parent. While working on a school project, a child created a mural that depicted American families. One of the families portrayed on the mural had two parents of the same sex. When a mother saw the student's rendition of family, the parent was outraged.

The mother immediately spoke to the principal asking the administrator to talk to the teacher about taking the wall painting down. The administrator explained to the parent that the school abided by a school covenant which was drafted by the school as a whole. According to this covenant, "Education in a democracy must promote understanding and respect for all people." Furthermore, the principal explained to the parent that the only way this shared agreement can be changed is through the same process in which it was created.

Another option for the parent, according to the school leader, was to petition the school improvement team. The parent chose not to do either. This incident caused the upset parent and others to see how committed the entire school was to the covenant. Thirty years later, the same belief system is still adhered to by the school.

School-wide guiding philosophies attributed to the success of students at more than twenty-six Texas schools who shared a common philosophy: "success for every student." This covenant was not just a mission, but it was illustrated in every aspect of schooling. Curriculum decisions, paraprofessional support, professional development, space allocation, school programs as well as remedial resources offered to students were driven by the daily mission of every student succeeding. Each student became a success in every area of the school. These Texas schools did whatever it took to ensure that all children were eventually high performers.

## Collaborative Relationships

Building relationships that have an ultimate goal of boosting student achievement in a school building mean exemplary schools. Exemplary schools understand that creating a cooperative environment is a must. Collaboration within an education institution allows students, parents, staff, and leadership to create relationships that carry out school objectives. Having the opportunity to identify and find solutions to issues proves to be crucial to all parties involved in collaborative relationships. The relationships must not be contrived. Giving students, staff, and volunteers a chance to contribute to school objectives in a meaningful manner proves to be effective.

Schools should never limit team configurations. Studies show that different types of teams can be successful in school environments. Collaborative relationships can involve grade-level teams, interdisciplinary teams, subject area teams, student support teams, leadership teams, and classroom management teams.

The key to creating effective collaborative relationships is focus. Concentrating on curriculum and student achievement issues proved to be advantageous for teachers in many studies. This insight is especially beneficial when instructors are allowed to collaborate on issues pertaining to instruction on a daily basis. Administration gave teachers ample time to collaborate on preparing lesson plans, resolving instructional issues, and learning together. Shared decision making benefits all parties involved. It makes participants feel valued as professional educators.

School leaders utilize different techniques in terms of gathering input from staff. On one hand, some administrators allow teachers and paraprofessionals to take part in the decision-making process through committees or governance structures. On the other hand, many principals simply ask for ideas or suggestions. Either way, shared decision making proved to be an attribute of high performing schools in many institutions. It is not just the leader who has a stake in decisions, but staff does as well.

Staff and leaders alike are affected by decisions made about the programs and operations of a school. Including staff in decision making helps a school become a more cohesive school environment. When the decision is collaborative, the whole team will work harder to see to it that goals are realized. All entities are willing to become a part of making it work.

The staff member's input becomes the most important aspect of the contribution to the school. Stakeholders will exceed their job responsibilities to achieve a goal that they helped to create. It is no longer just the leader's plan or the school's mission. A librarian might be willing to become a PTA representative, or a secretary might help children learn to read in an after-school program. It turns out to be personal when shared decision making is a part of a school environment. Collaborators are empowered with a sense of professional worth and purpose as a result.

### Family/School/Community Connection

Connectedness has proven to be a necessary ingredient in successful schools. This concept of connectedness to the school is not limited to families, but it includes community as well. Everyone wins when families and the community connect to the education institution in a meaningful manner. Students, staff, and community reap the benefits of working together to achieve the same goal. Children perform better when parents support the school environment. Parents begin to identify with staff in terms of understanding the educator's job. Staff report feeling more respected, and the community becomes a part of educating kids.

Effectiveness in educating students hinges on creating a climate of trust within collaborative working relationships. These relationships could include: students working with parents or community members, parents partnering with teachers, teachers collaborating with the principal, or staff members working together. Grade-level teams collaborate by considering student work and discussing what can be done, instruction-wise, to improve student performance.

Faculty might be encouraged to meet on the weekends to plan lessons and share ideas. Parent volunteers may work with students to improve reading fluency. The staff could be seen cooperatively making decisions with the principal. The key is building relationships that contribute to the effectiveness of the school.

Tension ensues when students are not connected to adults in a school building. Children can see that parents and staff care about helping kids succeed in a cooperative environment. Experiencing connectedness boosts student achievement and helps create a feeling of safety for students as well as staff. Within a cooperative environment, the leader makes it a priority to listen to staff and provide the resources necessary to do the best job.

Cooperative environments are also known as learning communities. Building learning communities might entail a school sharing space, partnering with local businesses to host a program where volunteers read to students, hosting a career development program utilizing parent volunteers, or incorporating family traditions through community members' input. These partnerships produce a positive end product with students as well as opportunities for staff and volunteers to make student achievement a reality.

Studies report that schools with a family-like atmosphere sets a pace within an environment that leads to enhanced student performance. Parents, administrators, students, and teachers alike enjoy the chance to share in the school vision. This sharing creates a sense of belonging to something meaningful. Class size, the culture of the students and the community the school serves, as well as school objectives influence the cohesiveness of a school environment.

Essentially, higher student performance is the ultimate goal. A climate of cooperativeness is born out of the following components: a guiding philosophy, collaborative relationships, and family/school/community connections. These three concepts lead to the ultimate goal.

## CAB: ACCOUNTABILITY

Accountability is the second characteristic found in successful schools. Basically, students and staff need to be held accountable in terms of meeting high standards. It becomes the responsibility of staff to set up an environment of accountability for students. In the same manner, the principal must initiate and maintain an accountability system in which staff can create an atmosphere of high expectations. Students must then rise up to the performance standards given the proper resources.

### Students

High performing schools generally share the following characteristic: high expectations through accountability. One example is how twenty-six Texas schools performed high on state achievement tests even though most of their students tended to be in the low socioeconomic background category. Teachers in these schools held children to high academic expectations regardless of the students' predicaments. No excuses were accepted and kids measured up to the high standards.

Another example of not making any excuses for students was seen in nine schools with an impoverished Limited in English Proficiency (LEP) largely Mexican-American populace. The instructors created an environment of academic accountability in which kids were taught how to be responsible for their own learning.

In both cases, the schools share a universal theme prevalent in excellent schools: every child succeeding. Successful schools plan in a way that each child can succeed. High performing educational institutions organize in a manner in which every child can be a success. Likewise, resources are utilized in accordance with contributing to the success of every student. Different schools embrace this theme in unique ways.

Four high schools decided to cancel all remedial classes and place teenagers in higher-level courses such as honors, International Baccalaureate (IB) or Advanced Placement (AP) classes. This move to author an environment of high standards almost completely closed the achievement gap at the four schools. Another high performing school incorporated high expectations in its school plan. Not only were all children enrolled in grade-level courses, but teachers did not utilize watered-down curricula or employ remedial skill-based activities.

Demanding courses are the first step in achieving high standards. The next step is holding all students to the same level of accountability. Lastly, learners must have the necessary resources available in order to meet the high expectations. Resources can come in any form. Successful schools do whatever is necessary to help scholars rise up to the high expectations. This may entail helping learners one-on-one, waking a student up in the morning because parents have already left for work, providing dinner for low-income families, teaching kids how to study, assisting students with reading, or offering grade-level math workshops.

Teachers play a major role in terms of attitude toward students' ability. When teachers believe that all students can learn, students usually learn. Maintaining such a high expectation means allowing this attitude that all kids can learn to drive the daily operations of a school. This attitude marks the difference between high performing and low performing schools. While a teacher at a low performing school may possess this attitude, it is generally an isolated case.

Unsuccessful schools tend to blame low performance on a lack of motivation on the part of students or on lack of interest on the part of parents. Teachers at low performing schools have the attitude that no matter what an instructor does, some students will never learn. However, an attitude of success is the norm at high performing schools. Successful schools do not stop until all children are learning.

It is perfectly fine to acknowledge that some children will require more assistance than other kids to learn. Along with this realization must come the understanding that more or different resources may be needed to help some struggling students attain high standards. Instead of focusing on memorization, a teacher may concentrate on thinking skills. A noisy classroom may allow an educator to offer fun learning activities for scholars.

Educators who teach high performing students rely on two vital techniques: continuous assessment of learners and utilization of different instructional strategies. One such reform that is widely used is referred to as Outcome Based Education (OBE). This method is contingent upon the idea that every student is capable of learning if taught accurately and given enough time to master the skill. The process includes teaching and then reteaching as well as testing and then retesting.

Exemplary institutions have assessed and reassessed students as a way of helping children achieve. Using the trial and error method has assisted teachers in choosing instructional strategies that yield results. Failure becomes a positive when it is viewed as a means of eliminating the techniques that do not yield results. Teachers tell students that failure is just a step toward reaching the goal. Educators and learners embrace failure so improved student achievement can become a reality.

Within this attitude of achievement, staff in high performing schools link high expectations to local, state, and national content standards. Content expectations are often confused with curriculum standards. Educators must be able to differentiate between the two types of standards. Basically, content benchmarks express what a student is expected to know or can do at a specific grade level. Curriculum standards, on the other hand, refer to the specifics of what happens in a classroom as teachers utilize various instructional strategies. Carrying out curriculum expectations will eventually move children toward meeting content standards.

"Developing number sense," for instance, is just one piece of a content standard. In order to fulfill this content benchmark, a student would, in the least, know how to write the same number in different ways. Writing these equivalents would be the curriculum standard. Consider this example: $½=.5=50\%$. The writing of these equivalent numbers help students to develop number sense. The instructional strategies and activities teachers use to meet the requirements of the content benchmark are curriculum standards. Curriculum expectations or learning objectives are often included in content standards under "in order to fulfill this benchmark, a scholar will…"

Content standards are abilities or skills people use on a daily basis in authentic life roles or in an academic setting. Developing number sense, for example, is an ability people utilize on a day-to-day basis in real life situations. One might need to figure out what 50 percent of a dollar is. It is not necessary to write it down, but a person would need to use number sense in order to do this. In a classroom environment, number sense proves to be essential in learning to count money, for example.

Aligning curriculum with content standards has become prevalent among educators since the curriculum expectations are generally consistent with content area knowledge at each grade level. This is why all students must meet state benchmarks irrespective of racial or financial background.

## Staff

Taking responsibility for student learning becomes the litmus test that determines whether high expectations flourish in a school environment. Students can only meet high standards when employees are not only held accountable, but when staff and leadership have created an accountability system that works for leadership, staff, and students.

Educators must address two vital needs in setting up an accountability system for students: improving student achievement and meeting state requirements. Faculty cannot afford to have tunnel vision and focus on one need. Whether it is classroom tests or state assessments, determining student weaknesses is a must. Instructional strategies and support services must be a means to an end. These techniques must be adjusted or eliminated when the needs of the students are not being met. Continuously assessing student knowledge plays a crucial role in achieving the two vital needs. Standardized tests as well as staff-created assessments can be tools in determining where children lack knowledge and skill.

The attitude that school employees have is just as important as the tools used to address student weaknesses. A prerequisite for taking responsibility for student learning is a switch in paradigm. This change in attitude became evident in a study that focused on ten elementary through high schools that serve low income and newly migrated students. These ten schools had consistently scored below state standards on state standardized tests. As a result, the schools were put on a list of low performing schools.

The realization that attitudes needed to change prompted staff to look at the situation differently than the educators had in the past. Instead of having the attitude that the students needed to help themselves, the faculty in these institutions decided to scaffold children until kids met state standards. The attitude change led the ten schools to being removed from the low performance list.

The professionalism that led the ten schools to getting off the low performance list is the same type of professionalism that must exist in all schools. Some schools that serve minority and low income students attribute student learning to professionalism. Teachers must simply do whatever it takes to create an environment of learning on a daily basis. This professional environment includes teacher competence, commitment to student learning, belief in students, concern for children, experience, and effectiveness in teaching kids.

An atmosphere of professionalism can only exist when leadership creates and maintains an effective accountability system. Leadership has proven to be an important factor among successful schools. Once administration sets up an accountability system, programs and curriculum must abide by the established guidelines. Since the accountability system targets the school objectives, student achievement can be more readily accomplished.

When staff has access to practical professional development, improved student achievement generally follows. Administration is ultimately responsible for being an instructional facilitator who provides, sets up, or points employees to staff development that connects to what a school wants to accomplish in the classroom. As part of the accountability system, a leader must, in the least, establish a way for employees to monitor their staff development.

Like teachers, leaders must be willing to do whatever is necessary to help students achieve success. Actions of principals that illustrate this concept include one administrator who facilitated a field trip of faculty members to high and low performing schools so staff could differentiate between techniques that work and strategies that do not. The same principal drove employees throughout the area that students live so the staff could know firsthand what issues kids deal with outside of school. He also led a book study on poverty to help staff understand the challenges poor children face.

Another administrator collaborated with staff to research programs with proven success. The school ultimately implemented the programs. One school focused on doing a year-long study in which faculty circulated through a different grade level each month to gather pertinent data about strategies that work. The sharing of this information proved to be very beneficial.

Principals know that expectations must be high in order to achieve an effective accountability system. The standards need to be high enough for a school to perform at its maximum capacity. Leadership, faculty, and students alike must be held accountable within an environment that embraces student learning. Fundamentally, each party has a job to do to guarantee that student achievement happens while functioning as one entity.

Chapter 7

# CAB: BOUNDLESSNESS

The last concept in the CAB education model is Boundlessness: data-driven evaluation. This means that a school operates in a mode of continuous growth and improvement through self-evaluation.

## Data-Driven School-wide Evaluation

Schools make no excuses when practicing boundlessness. Regardless of the type of population a school serves, schools practicing boundlessness are constantly looking for unique ways to operate in an atmosphere of discovery that evaluates the different entities within the school. Seeking improvement in these schools does not necessarily originate from leadership. The mode of perpetual growth comes from the individual. Students desire to improve skills. Teachers seek out opportunities to help them become more effective instructors. Leaders search out ways to grow as an example to faculty and students.

Self-imposed evaluation occurs in schools that practice boundlessness even when test scores are high. These schools have a tendency to focus on school improvement more than schools not meeting state benchmarks. Continuous growth is just another aspect of schooling to each party within the school. The attitude in such schools is that improvement is a must. This way of thinking means that schools practicing boundlessness make a commitment that school decisions arise out of careful data analysis.

Data analysis may consist of a group of teachers coming together throughout the summer to analyze disaggregative data to identify areas students need help in. This level of commitment caused one junior high school to put each student on an individual achievement plan much like the Individual Education Plan (IEP).

Gathering and analyzing information to make decisions or choosing instructional strategies is just the beginning for schools practicing boundlessness. Such schools might exhibit information throughout the school building in the form of visual aids or graphic representations. Displaying data in this fashion on a regular basis places staff in the same continuous mode of growth and learning as students.

Just as evaluating data contributes to keeping staff in a mode of constant growth, the utilization of data is also helpful in making professional development decisions. Data-driven evaluation is useful in connecting staff development to learning as well. One example is noted in a study of twelve schools that serve predominately low income students. In results-driven environments, administrators and faculty acknowledged the link between professional development and student learning. Gathering information and analyzing data became crucial steps in the process of linking staff development to student achievement.

Honest evaluation naturally enhances boundlessness. In one school, the analysis of data such as student work, principal observations, and assessments led to resolving an issue. Students were not learning an essential skill so leadership allocated resources to address the lack through professional development. Staff ultimately learned which instructional strategies better equipped faculty to teach the skill.

Basically, boundlessness incorporates certain characteristics that prove to be a natural progression in data-driven evaluation. These attributes include operating in a mode of perpetual growth and learning through gathering and analyzing data. Staff, students, and leadership are willing participants in the process of evaluating to improve student achievement and connect professional development to learning. In order to do this, faculty must be trained how to use and analyze pertinent data so student achievement and staff development can be enhanced.

# References

Bailey, C. A. (2007). *A guide to qualitative field research* (2nd ed.). Thousand Oaks, CA: Pine Forge Press.
Bennett, N., & Harris, A. (1999). Hearing truth from power? Organisation theory, school effectiveness and school improvement. *School Effectiveness and School Improvement 10*(4), 533–50.
Berg, B. L. (2007). *Qualitative research methods for the social sciences* (6th ed.). Boston: Allyn and Bacon.
Billig, S. H., et al. (2005). *Closing the achievement gap: Lessons from successful schools.* Washington, DC: U.S. Department of Education, Office of Vocational and Adult Education.
Blair, L. (2000, April). Strategies for change: Implementing a comprehensive school reform program, part 1. *CSRD Connections, 1*(2), 2–13.
Bogotch, I. E. (2001). Precipitating consequences in educational leadership: Diffusion, activism, and accountability. Florida Atlantic University. (ERIC Document Reproduction Service No. ED454584).
Bosker, R. J. & Witziers, Bob (1995). *A meta analytical approach regarding school effectiveness: The true size of school effects and the effect size of educational leadership.* Enschede: University of Twente, Division of Education Administration. (ERIC Document Reproduction Service No. ED392147).
Carroll, J. B. (1963). A model of school learning. *Teachers College Record, 64*, 722–33.
Carter., S. C. (1999). *No excuses: Seven principals of low-income schools who set the standard for high achievement.* Washington, DC: The Heritage Foundation.
*Characteristics of successful schools* (2nd ed.) (2000, August). (Report Bull01001). Madison, Wisconsin: State Department of Public Instruction.
Connell, N. (1996). *Getting off the list: School improvement in New York City.* New York: Educational Priorities Panel.
Corallo, C. & Mcdonald, D. (2001). *What works with low-performing schools: A review of research literature on low-performing schools.* Charleston, WV: Appalachia Educational Laboratory.
Cotton, K. (2000). *The schooling practices that matter most.* Portland, OR: Northwest Regional Educational Laboratory.
Craig, J., et al. (2005), *A case study of six high-performing schools in Tennessee.* Charleston, WV: Appalachia Educational Laboratory (AEL), Inc.
Creemers, B. P. M. (1993, January). *Towards a theory on educational effectiveness.* Paper presented at the Annual Meeting of the International Congress for School Effectiveness and Improvement, Norrkoping, Sweden.

Creemers, B. P. M. (1997, March). *Visions that work: A further elaboration of the comprehensive model of educational effectiveness*. Paper presented at Annual Meeting of the American Educational Research Association, Chicago, IL.

Daggett, W. R. (2005, June). *Successful schools: From research to action plans*. Paper presented at the Model Schools Conference.

Doyle, L. H. (1997, October). *Leadership and teaching in four schools with varied organizational structures and social contexts*. Paper presented at the University Council for Educational Administration, Orlando, FL.

Edmonds, R. (1979). Effective schools for the urban poor. *Educational Leadership*. 37(1), 15–24.

Ellis, S., et al. (2004). *Case studies and cross-case analysis of promising practices in selected urban public school districts in Massachusetts*. Hadley, MA: University of Massachusetts Donahue Institute.

Fouts, J. T. (2003). *A decade of reform: A summary of research findings on classroom, school, and district effectiveness in Washington state* (Report No. 3). Lynwood, WA: Seattle Pacific University, Washington School Research Center.

Glickman, Carl D. (2002). The courage to lead. *Educational Leadership, 59*, 41–44.

Goldstein, J., Kelemen, M. & Koski, W. (1998, April). *Reconstitution in theory and practice: The experience of San Francisco*. Paper presented at the Annual Meeting of the American Educational Research Association, San Diego, CA.

Griffith, J. (2003). Schools as organizational models: Implications for examining school effectiveness. *The Elementary School Journal, 104*(1), 29–47.

Hair, D., Kraft, B., & Allen, A. (2001). *National Staff Development Council Project ADVANCE mini-grant: Louisiana Staff Development Council's end of grant report*. Baton Rouge, LA: Louisiana Staff Development Council.

Henderson, A. T., & Mapp, K. L. (2002). *A new wave of evidence: The impact of school, family, and community connections on student achievement. Annual synthesis 2002*. Austin, TX: National Center for Family and Community Connections with Schools, Southwest Education Development Laboratory.

Huang, S. L., Waxman, H. & Wang, M. (1995, April). *Comparing school-based environment of high- and low-performing inner city schools*. Paper presented at the Annual Meeting of the American Educational Research Association, San Francisco, CA.

Irwin, J.W. & Farr, W. (2004). Collaborative school communities that support teaching and learning. *Reading and Writing Quarterly, 20*, 343–63.

Joint Legislative Audit and Review Commission (JLARC) of the Virginia General Assembly. (2004). *Review of factors and practices associated with school performance in Virginia*. Richmond, VA: Author.

Jones, M. S., & Ross, E. F. (1994, January). *School improvement: a case study. An effective schools framework for partnerships in systemic reform*. Paper presented at the Annual Meeting of the International Congress for School Effectiveness and Improvement, Victoria, Australia.

Kannapel, P. J., et al. (2005). *Inside the black box of high-performing high poverty schools*. KY, Lexington: Prichard Committee for Academic Excellence.

Kaufman R., Herman, J., & Watters, K. (2002). *Educational planning: Strategic, tactical, and operational*. Lanham, MD: Scarecrow Press, Inc.

Kendall, J. S., & Marzano, R. J. (1994). *The systematic identification and articulation of content standards and benchmarks: Update* (Contract RP91002005). Aurora, CO: Mid-Continent Regional Educational Lab.

Keyes, M. W., & Udvari-Solner, A. (1999, April). *Chronicles of administrative leadership toward inclusive reform: We're on the train and we've left the station, but we haven't gotten to the next stop*. Paper presented at the Annual Meeting of the American Educational Research Association, Montreal, Quebec, Canada.

Kull, J. A., et al. (1994, April). *Mathematics and science reform through school/university collaboration: Fables from the field in four middle/junior high schools*. Paper presented at the Annual Meeting of the American Educational Research Association, New Orleans, Louisiana.

Kyriakides, L., Campbell, R. J., & Gagatsis, A. (2000). The significance of the classroom effect in primary schools: An application of Creemers' comprehensive model of educational effectiveness. *School Effectiveness and School Improvement, 11*(4), 501–29.

Lein, L., Johnson, J. F., Jr., & Ragland, M. (1997). *Successful Texas school-wide programs: Research study results, school profiles and voices of practitioners and parents.* University of Texas: The Charles A. Dana Center; Support for Texas Academic Renewal.

Lockwood, A. T. (1996). *Productive schools: perspectives from research and practice.* Oakbrook, IL: North Central Regional Educational Lab.

Marzano, R. J. (2003). *What works in schools: Translating research into action.* Alexandria, VA: ASCD.

McGee, G. (2003). Closing Illinois' achievement gap: Lessons from the "golden spike" high poverty high-performing schools. *Journal of Education for Students Placed at Risk 9*(2), 97–125.

Meehan, M. L., & Cowley, K. S. (2003, January). *A study on low-performing schools, high performing schools, and high-performing learning communities.* Paper presented at the Hawaii International Conference on Education, Waikiki, HI.

Moscovici, H. & Alfaro-Varela, G. (1993, April). *Collaborative efforts in school culture.* Paper presented at the Annual Meeting of the American Educational Research Association, Atlanta, Georgia.

Newmann, F. M, Wehlage, G. G (1995). *Successful school restructuring: A report to the public and educators* (Contract No. R117Q0000595). Washington, DC: American Federation of Teachers; Alexandria, VA: ASCD; Alexandria, VA: National Association of Elementary School Principals; Reston, VA: The National Association of Secondary School Principals.

North Central Regional Educational Laboratory, (2004). *Case studies of high-performing, high-technology schools: Final research report on schools with predominantly low-income, African-American, or Latino Student populations* (Contract No. ED01CO0011) . Naperville, Illinois: Learning Point Associates.

Picucci, A., Brownson, A., Kahlert, R., & Sobel, A. (2002). *Driven to succeed: High performing, high-poverty, turnaround middle schools. Volume I: Cross-case analysis of high-performing, high-poverty, turnaround middle schools.* Washington, DC: U.S. Department of Education.

Reeves, D. B. (2005). *The 90/90/90 schools: A case study.* Denver, CO: Center for Performance Assessment.

Sanders, B. (2009). *A Case Study of Two Alternative Community-based Schools in Portland, Oregon* (doctoral dissertation). George Fox University: Newberg, Oregon. http://summit.worldcat.org/title/case-study-of-two-alternative-community-based-schools-in-portland-oregon/oclc/680822715&referer=brief_results

Sanders, B. (2010). Themes found in high performing schools: The CAB model. *Academic Leadership: The Online Journal, 8*(2). http://www.academicleadership.org/.

Scribner, A. P., & Scribner, J. D. (2001), High performing schools serving Mexican American students: What they can teach us. *ERIC Digest , December*, 1–9.

Shields, P. M., et al. (1995). *Improving schools from the bottom up: From effective schools to restructuring, Final report* (SRI Project HSU-1609). Washington, DC: U.S. Government Printing Office.

Simons, K. A., & Curtis, P. A. (2007). Connecting with communities: Four successful schools. *YC Young Children, 62*(2), 12–20.

Strauss, A., & Corbin, J. (1990). *Basics of qualitative research: Grounded theory procedures and techniques.* Newbury Park, CA: Sage.

Taylor, B. O. (1990). *Case studies in effective schools research.* Dubuque, IA: Kendall/Hunt Publishing Company.

Teddlie, C. & Reynolds, D. (2001). Countering the critics: Responses to recent criticisms of school effectiveness research. *School Effectiveness and School Improvement 12*(1), 41-82.

Texas Education Agency (TEA) (2000). *The Texas successful school study: Quality education for Limited English Proficient (LEP) students.* Austin: Texas Education Agency.

Thiessen, D., & Anderson, S. E. (1999). *Getting into the habit of change in Ohio schools: The cross-case study of 12 transforming learning communities.* Columbus, OH: Department of Education.

Trimble, S. (2002). Common elements of high-performing, high poverty middle schools. *Middle School Journal, 33*(4), 7–16.

U. S. Department of Education (USDE) (1999). *Hope for urban education: A study of nine High-performing, high-poverty, urban elementary schools.* Washington, DC: Author. http://www.ed.gov/pubs/urbanhope/.

Wong, K., Hedges, L., Borman, G., & D'Agostino, J. V. (1996). *Prospects: Special analyses, Final report* (Contract No. EA94084101). Washington DC: Department of Education, Office of the Under Secretary.

Yin, R. K. (2003). *Case study research design and methods* (3$^{rd}$ ed.). Thousand Oaks: Sage Publications.

# Index

accountability, 47; in leadership, 47, 49, 50, 53, 58; with teachers, 47, 54, 55, 56, 57, 58
boundlessness, 61; in data-driven evaluation, 61, 62, 63, 64, 65, 69

collaborative relationships: student collaborations, 32; in family/school/community connections, 40, 41, 42
cooperativeness 7; in collaborative relationships, 7, 29–30; in family/school/community connections, 7; as a school-wide guiding philosophy, 7, 25–26

example of a vision Statement, 14
example of final school-wide guiding philosophy, 17
example of school-wide guiding philosophy stemming from vision statement, 14
examples of collaborative relationships, 30–31
examples of family/school/community connections, 40–41

interview with a school administrator, 62–63
interview with a school principal, 22, 58

Mission statement: mission ojectives, 18–19, 20, 26; examples of mission objectives, 20

school-wide collaborative relationships: mission objectives, 36
school-wide guiding philosophy: example of Mission Statement, 17
school-wide guiding philosophy: *see also* Student Bill of Rights, 17; in collaborative relationships, 33, 35, 36; as a mission statement, 26; as a vision statement, 11–12, 13, 26
school-wide guiding philosophy, 10; mission statement, 14–15, 17
staff Accountability, 48

Student Bill of Rights, 17

www.ingramcontent.com/pod-product-compliance
Lightning Source LLC
Chambersburg PA
CBHW070337230426
43663CB00011B/2359